This book is possible because
David, Matthew, John and Barbara Hopkins
grew up and left Mary Ellen with nothing else
to do.

"Yes, I'll make you a quilt because I love you and yes, you can sit on the quilt!!!!!"

For my boys whose vans never seem to have a working heater, for my daughter who is currently supporting the nail polish industry while sitting cross-legged on the bed with her friends, and for my friends who drink cocoa in bed - yes, **it's okay if you sit on my quilt.**

Why? Because I've learned secrets about cutting and piecing that make it possible for me to make quilts in a fraction of the time you would expect without sacrificing design. In fact, when you finish this book I believe you will have so many exciting design and technique ideas that nothing will keep you from making quilts.

All of The Indispensible Patchwork Patterns in this workbook are made up entirely of squares, right triangles and strips.

Included are secrets about patchwork squares that no one ever tells you, secret ways to: look at them, use them, mark them, cut them, sew them, and set them.

One secret is that several have been redrafted and interpreted in squares and triangles, eliminating more difficult shapes so that our secret techniques can be employed.

This technique of designing quilts will especially appeal to you if, like me, you can remember third grade. Do you remember having a little resentment for the girl who could draw a horse? A perfect horse. Not just in art class, but on her notebook cover and scratch pads. Well, I remember and I also remember how excited I was when they handed out the graph paper and I started coloring razzle-dazzle geometric designs!

As we progress through this book, you'll be introduced to the joys of graph paper. This book is intended for you to actually work in and to add your own work pages. And I don't hold grudges. You're welcome to read on, even if you can draw horses.

1

**Checklist on how to get that
"Art School Graduate" look:**

1.   Put it on the diagonal
2.   Use connector blocks
3.   Remember the famous 9-Patch set up
4.   Try positive - negative themes
5.   Float
6.   Clean - up
7.   Add on to finish the design
8.   Shade in as though it were one block
9.   Barn Raising Set
10. Mirror Image

Before we begin, it is important to understand that the whole point of this book is to be able to apply artistic principles to create beautiful quilts without having to go to school to learn art theory - and to do it with ease! To this end, this book will demonstrate the principles listed above so you too can easily create wonderful designs to amaze your friends and relatives and leave them awestruck at your generosity when you give away those quilts which you "slaved over for months and months." Whatever you do, don't let them see this book! Now, let's get started!

Starting at Square One

First of all, let's get one thing straight. This is not a step-by-step "how to" quilt-from-beginning-to-end book.. There are lots of those.

This is an *attitude adjustment* quilt book. Too many people think that a quilt must be painstakingly planned and drug out for years of piecing and perfect quilting. This is not to put down the masterpiece quilt. It's to say every quilt need not be one. So roll up your sleeves and start.

Why do we make a quilt?

1. To keep someone we love warm.

2. To create something of our own choosing. To say "This is ME!"

3. It's a reason to play with all those colors and patterns and designs we have floating around in our heads.

4. And let's face it - for those of us who are fabricologists, it's a chance to be with what we love.

5. It's just plain therapeutic. It's a pleasant pace to keep - your hands are busy, your mind is playing with designs - and still you can watch television, talk with the family and not get mixed up.

6. And don't overlook the satellite bonuses - like being wined and dined by someone who wants you to make a quilt - and the fact that it does wonders for your reputation.

You do not need to be a sewer to embark on this road of love. If you are one of the many who definitely did not shine in Home Ec - not to worry. I consider sewing about 4th down the list of what you need to know. The sewing is simple - just sew straight ahead in a straight line using a simple running stitch. When you're on the machine, you really don't need to touch anything - just stitch straight ahead!

The traditional idea of quiltmaking is a cut-each-separate-piece and sew-each-separate-piece method. In this book we will introduce you to quick cutting, piecing before cutting, etc. I really can't believe that this is a novel way of piecing. In fact I remember my aunt doing some similar things. And take a look at Seminole patchwork - almost entirely based on sewing strips together, then cutting and resewing in a different arrangement.

I have a theory that our forebears learned quick techniques too, but perhaps the Puritan ethic made them keep it to themselves rather than "admit" to shortcuts. Busy work for work's sake just is not in my scheme of things. (Does a tomato taste any better if you dig the ground with a stick instead of a shovel?) So I refuse to be intimidated by the idea that Grandma did it piece by piece and therefore it's better. I hope she really did know my techniques. If you feel the same, keep going.

Some common sense feelings about fabrics

About 100% cotton - well, I wish every print and every shade that I wanted to use would be made of cotton - it's so terrific to work with - but they just aren't. My first priority is for color, so yes, I'll use blends. Blends vary so much. Try to stay clear of the wibbly-wobbly ones, you have to slow way down on your sewing speed. However, there is one terrific dull gray green blend that wobbles as though it were alive, but I'll still hassle it because I'm in love with that particular shade. Experience is, to me, the best teacher. If you are having a particular problem, and one fabric is a blend, you may decide to change. It is more important to stay in the same **weight** of fabric. A heavier, coarser fabric will weaken the lighter fabric that it is seamed to. And yes, if you can, I really believe cotton is much simpler to

work with. It eases in patchwork better and the edges can be turned under easily for applique.

Pre-shrinking and washing all fabric first is, of course, the safest way to go. However, when I know I've got a top quality piece of goods, I've skipped this and not gotten into trouble. **But**, the selvage is always bad news. Never use it. The threads in the selvage are not always the same threads as in the fabric and they can draw up something awful. If I do want to shrink something first, I prefer to immerse it in hot water, blot it in a towel and iron it dry. That way it is a lot easier to mark and cut. It's not as limp as fabric that's had the full wash and dry routine.

The best way to store your fabric is by color. And all together. I have known women who will suspend shelves from their bathroom ceiling, just to be able to usurp the linen closet. Pin a long slip of paper to each piece of fabric stating the amount and then each time you use some of it, subtract the amount used. This is a habit you'll be thankful you started.

Do not store any of your fabric in plastic bags - you think you're keeping them dust free, but actually you're rotting them out. That fabric has got to breathe. Cover the stacks with old sheets, tablecloths or curtains instead.

Are you a compulsive buyer of fabric? So am I and I felt very guilty indeed, until I opened my quilt shop and found **hundreds of others** in the same club!! Since there are endless ways of rationalizing this buying habit and since none of us feel the slightest inclination to overcome it - just carry on. I found the offensive position the best. Do not try to apologize or explain it - just raise your eyebrows and **assume** that your accuser is off beat.

Downhome tips on color

First of all I think color in quilts is virtually impossible to "teach". The color wheel doesn't really help when you're working with quilts. The color wheel has one solid chip of color next to another. Not at all what we do with printed fabrics. So over the years, I've developed some attitudes about color. I'd like you to consider incorporating them.

Forget about trying to match everything

Say, for instance, you're putting a little narrow green frame around the center of your quilt top. There is absolutely no need to match it to the shade of green that is the leaf color of one of your flowered prints. Instead it should be a green that looks good with the whole quilt. Stand back and put in some color that looks good with the whole quilt. Not all this little tiny-matchy-uppy.

Learn that clash is not always a negative word. Rusts, browns and golds are the safest combination. But to avoid the ho-hums, try to have one fabric that "clashes" - a wine or black for instance.

Within a color family, shades of red are the easiest to combine. That is, red with an orange cast can be used with a blue red, cherry red, etc. more easily than hues of other colors. So when I say all reds clash well, I hope you understand.

Blues are probably the most difficult hues to combine. You put a bunch of blues together and nothing happens. They seem to cancel each other out. I suggest going for a "prominent" blue look, while using other colors as well. Using a bit of purple, violet or mauve will add a lot of "color" to your blues. Navy is the easiest of the blues because it gives a more graphic look.

Contrary to popular belief, black is bright, gay and sparkling. Honest. It will perk things up like you couldn't believe.

A little piece of green will sure add some spark to almost any quilt. I've been quoted as saying, "Don't show me a quilt that doesn't have green, purple or black in it somewhere." Again I admit it's not orthodox color theory, but start looking. The easiest thing to have happen is that you'll get a boring quilt because you're afraid to try something different.

Trying to make a quilt for a certain room all the time can sure squelch you. Let go and just make a gorgeous quilt.

The Importance of Standing Back

When selecting fabrics for a quilt, it is always a good idea to keep moving back and looking at alternatives for a distance. Very few people see a quilt or a quilted project of any kind from 18". The effect of the combined fabrics from several feet away becomes crucial to the selection.

Both colors and patterns play tricks on your selection when you stand back. If standing back isn't convenient, at least squint.

Mixing types of Designs - Almost as important as color!

Much of the charm of quilts is the interplay of individual fabric designs. It is virtually impossible to categorize all fabrics into just a few types, but let's discuss some of the most common.

Small, dense designs

a. If the objects in a dense design are all one color family, they substitute well for a solid. They add variety safely. Be careful if the fabric is very dark with lots of white. It will look much lighter or "washed out" from a few feet away.

b. Small, dense designs with multiple colors take more thought and care. It's especially important to stand back. The colors may cancel each other out completely, or an unexpected color may dominate.

Random designs

Random designs are difficult to find, but wonderful to use. They don't allow the fabric to develop surprise secondary patterns. They don't get boring. Each small piece cut from a random design can look completely different. Small random designs make especially nice background fabrics.

Open and airy prints

These designs are usually a more delicate pattern, spread out but still connected with a thin, viny detail. They provide wonderful relief to other fabric designs.

Large designs

Anything between small and gigantic may classify as large.

a. A large, dense design is a very easy way to introduce many colors. The shapes are big enough to see each color separately. This allows you to emphasize a specific color with the other fabrics you choose.

b. Large airy designs with lots of background color between motifs become the same as gigantic prints.

Gigantic designs

To many quilters, any design element larger than 3" is gigantic. I like large designs for the very same reason most people don't use them. Cut into small pieces, a gigantic design can cut into many different colors and patterns. It's like creating your own random designs! Used throughout a quilt, the fabric ties the quilt together, but adds so much movement!

Special Fabrics

Pindots & Polkadots

Pindots and polkadots are not the same thing. Pindots are so small, you can't measure their diameter. Pindots, or microdots, have become a mainstay in the last few years. They may well be used as a solid with more interest. However, from 10 feet away, the dot is usually not visible.

Polkadots come in every measurable size. Generally, the smaller they are, the easier they are to use.

Checks, Tattersalls, Plaids & other Geometrics

When small, these can be a neat, tailored little pattern that really catches the eye. They can be used to highlight a certain section of a quilt pattern. Generally, the larger they are, the more unwieldy to use.

Stripes

Recognizable stripes can often be used very effectively as borders or to add dramatic movement to a quilt design. The excitement they can add when well-used makes the extra thought worthwhile.

Non-recognizable stripes are those fabrics that have designs in a row. Sometimes, this only becomes visible as you use the fabric. A printed "in a row" pattern can often be used like a subtle stripe but can also mar a quilt if not cut carefully.

Remember - mixing types of designs is probably just as important as color in quilt design. The easiest trap is to use all tiny prints.

Getting Ready to Mark and Cut — Quick Style

Before I indulged in the acrylic rules, I bought large poster boards (22" wide at stores that carry office supplies) and cut them precisely and carefully into the width of strips I needed. If you're not accurate here, you're dead. These strips wear down and must be remade often. You'll see why we need these later.

For all my marking, I use (hold your breath) a black thin-line Bic ball point!! The scissors cut right through this tiny thin line - it disappears and being able to **see** that line makes cutting more accurate.

I only mark the light fabric, then slip the **dark** fabric underneath and cut all at once. I always mark with another piece of fabric underneath so it won't wibble-wobble on the table top.

A decent pair of sewing scissors will cut through 4 thicknesses with no problem. If you're hooked on this stuff, you might consider going for the big time. A really good pair of scissors will cut 6-8 thicknesses with no distortion. Now slow down when you're cutting and look to see if the bottom layers are distorting. If they are, start pinning here and there. Hold your scissors straight up so you don't cut at an angle.

Some markers (I use the term "markers" rather than "quilters" because you may be lucky enough to hook someone else around you into being the "marker" - a plea of helplessness works great with most men) are able to use the horizontal templates in conjunction with a cutting board marked in one-inch lines. Test yourself first. Personally, I don't do well at all on it.

And yes, I cut strips on the crosswise grain.

A super alternative to scissors is the rotary cutter. (If you haven't seen one, it resembles a pizza cutter.)

Along with the rotary cutter you will need a cutting mat and at least one clear acrylic rule marked in $1/_8$" increments. (A 6" x 12" Salem Rule is an excellent choice.) Make sure the cutter edge is next to the rule when cutting. Get a good demonstration and you'll see the benefits of the rotary cutter if you are making lots of strips.

About Sewing

Usually your sewing machine foot is about $1/_4$" from the edge of the fabric to the needle so all you'll need to do is line up the edge of the foot with the edge of the fabric. If your machine's foot isn't $1/_4$", not to worry as long as you use the same foot for the entire quilt so all of the seam allowances are the same width. Your presser foot is your PPM , Personal Private Measurement (discussed onpage 10).

Set your stitch slightly larger than you use for ordinary sewing. I like it about $3/_4$ of the way to "basting" or 8-9 stitches per inch.

I sew all my seams with natural colored thread. It's stronger because there's no dye in it. If you buy it by the cone there is a tremendous saving.

I never back stitch. You will always be crossing a line of stitching with another line. It's just too time consuming, and miserable to rip out.

About ironing

Ironing a lot is great. It will keep your work neater, cleaner and more accurate. A terrific investment is a light iron. Try to find one light enough and small enough to use on a stool placed near your seat or the arm of an overstuffed chair. Wherever possible, seams should be ironed to one side, towards the darker fabric. There are still times when only opened seams will work.

Remember, you are all powerful with that hot iron! It is possible to iron a perfectly cut square of fabric into a lopsided parallelogram, never to be square again. **Don't iron aggressively! Just press.**

Feel free to change your original plan

While I don't push long drawn out plans for a quilt, everyone has an idea or a sketch or graph paper design when they start a quilt. Remember, it's not binding.

If you've gotten carried away with too wild of a color scheme in your blocks, change your game plan a little bit and tie the whole thing together with matching window pane strips.

You've made just 4 blocks and don't want to do anymore? Put the 4 together and use them for the center of a medallion quilt.

By the way, medallion quilt tops are grand for tablecloths. Use flannel for the inside layer and you'll have a minimum of quilting to do.

Center of the medallion not too red-hot? Use it on a table where there's always a centerpiece sitting on top of it.

Get the message? **Always** use something you've done **somewhere.**

Don't despair because there is no more of a certain fabric available and you didn't get enough. So one block will have to be different - big deal. You can always say you wanted that one block to symbolize something in your life.

Some people call if Fudging It, Winging It, Flying by the Seat of Your Pants. I like to think of it as flexible, open to knew ideas.

It also keeps more people you love snuggled under quilts and cuts your flop count to zero.

Glossary

Fabricologist - one who collects and understands fabric
Muckle - to mix up fabrics
PPF - Personal Private Friend
PPM - Personal Private Measurement
PPP - Personal Private Pages (which you're certainly going to have, aren't you)
PPR - Personal Private Rule
PPT - Perfect Pieced Triangle
PPV - Personal Private Variation
Whomp - To cut segments with a rotary cutter
Whizzy Whacker - Rotary Cutter

Lots of patterns that are traditionally made up of parallelograms, trapezoids and other shapes can actually be broken down into just squares and right triangles, simply by super-imposing a grid over them.

The whole trick is either in your mind's eye or by little dotted lines super-imposed in a grid over the pattern.

How to Mark, Cut and Sew Your Perfect Pieced Triangles the Accurate and Hassle Free Way

Without having to mark the dark fabric, first determine what size you want the finished size of this unit to be.

Example: 1 1/2" finished square

Now add one whole inch to this desired finished size, which would make it 2 1/2".

Lay two different fabrics right sides together, lighter colored fabric on top. It's not good to use pieces of fabric larger than 18" x 22", because it gets too unwieldy. We quilters call this size a fat quarter. A fat eighth would be 18" x 11", which is the size I always use.

Using your Salem Rule and a fine-line black ballpoint pen, mark a 2 1/2" grid of squares on the light fabric.

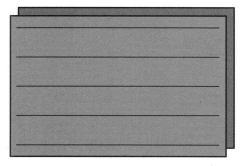

Step 1: Draw horizontal lines.

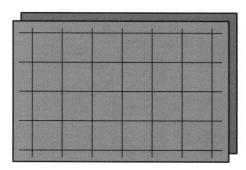

Step 2: Draw vertical lines.

Use 2nd color for diagonal lines

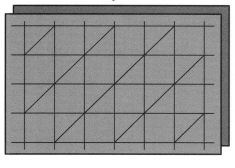

Step 3: Draw diagonal lines in every other square starting in one corner.

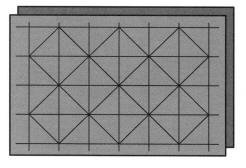

Step 4: Now draw diagonal lines in opposite direction in empty squares that are left.

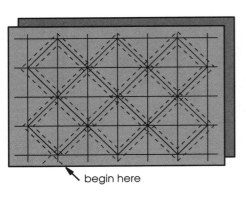

begin here

Step 5: Stitch in one continuous line using the same side of your presser foot all the time. This helps solve the problem of touchy tension and clears up one - directional fabrics.

Iron before cutting

Bonus: No stitches in the corners of cut triangles!!

There is just no way around it, these seams are going to have to be pressed before you use them! Ironing them open is a drag, but for some patterns you'll have to, otherwise you'll get too many thicknesses at one point. But for 75% of the patterns, ironing the way the fabric wants to go is what you'll do.

Square lines are critical lines

Press the drawn and stitched triangles before cutting. Cut on all the drawn lines. Before opening and using, be sure to clip the corners off. If you don't, this excess will drive you crazy!

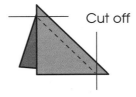

Cut off

Iron open

The Grid

What do we mean by the "Grid"?

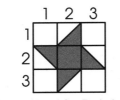

Sample of 3 - Patch Star

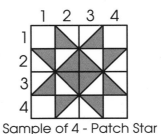

Sample of 4 - Patch Star

Graph paper lines are a grid. The pattern is counted by the number of squares across and the number of squares down.

I like working on four squares to the inch graph paper. If copying white graph paper with blue lines on a copy machine, the graph lines will drop out.

Each square on the grid (or graph paper) will be either a solid square:

Or a right triangle:

Size

You determine what size each little square will equal in its finished state.

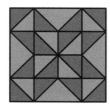

Example: This 4 - Patch Star would be approximately
6" square if each square equals 1 $\frac{1}{2}$" finished
8" square if each square equals 2" finished
10" square if each square equals 2 $\frac{1}{2}$" finished

Now start getting your eye to see the breakdown. In the example below, you will notice that patterns having parallelograms break down into two right triangles.

Pinwheel
Block #42

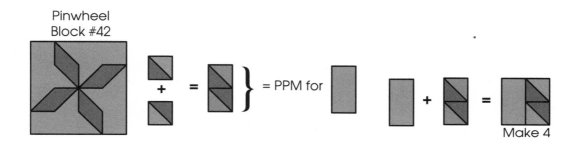

By building your block in this "Twosy - Foursy" way, your piecing will be much more efficient. By sewing blocks instead of rows, you eliminate many seams. The efficiency of this method is especially apparent when making a large quilt.

Right Triangles and Squares

You will find many patterns that are not presented as right triangles or squares but you will still be able to super - impose a grid over them and come out with square and right triangles without the least bit of distortion . Here is Salem, Oregon:

Or you will see a pattern you just love from a distance or in a photo that doesn't show the stitching lines of the block. Just squint and close one eye and try to count out even squares across. If you haven't any graph paper handy in your patchwork totebag, you must draw a rough grid and then fill in the squares and right triangles or you'll never be able to copy it once you get home. Here is a darling little Ribbon Bow:

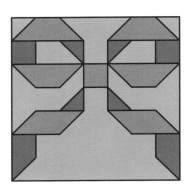

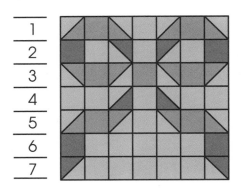

How to Mark and Cut the Squares

Now that you have your diagonal squares 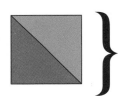 the next step is to cut out the plain squares ▢

Lay your Salem Rule on top of your pressed PPT and measure **CAREFULLY** (raw edge to raw edge). **This raw edge to raw edge measurement is your PPM.** With the Salem, you can clearly see perfect eighth inches and even half-eighth inches.

The following diagrams illustrate what we mean by your Personal Private Measurement (PPM).

This measurement raw edge to raw edge, which is your PPM, gives you the measurement for your plain square. Cut a strip this measurement, then cut your squares as illustrated:

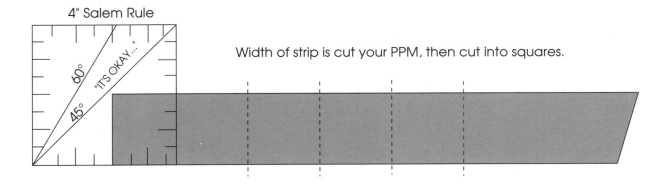

4" Salem Rule

Width of strip is cut your PPM, then cut into squares.

More PPM'S

Let's say you need a to go into You need to sew two

PPT's together: press, then measure raw edge to raw edge (your PPM), }

and cut a strip this width. (Refer to page 10.) Now you just whizzy whack off the squares for the block ! You must always make your smallest blocks first, and build from there.

Anatomy of a Sewing Breakdown

Larger blocks may be broken down into units instead of rows as you can see in this diagram of The Bear's Paw.

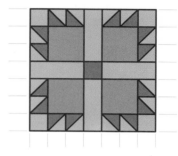

Each = 1 ½", makes a 10 ½" block.

 = PPM for

 + + =

+

 + = = = = 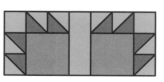 ⬅ Make 4

 + +  = ⬅ Make 2

+ + = ⬅ Make 1

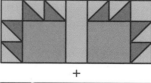

+

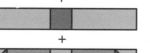

+

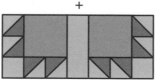 =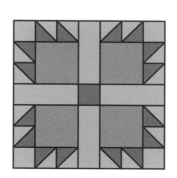

11

Become familiar with the breakdown. Study a pattern carefully to find the easiest way to piece it, with the fewest number of pieces. If you spend a few moments working out a pattern on graph paper, you'll save yourself a lot of grief.

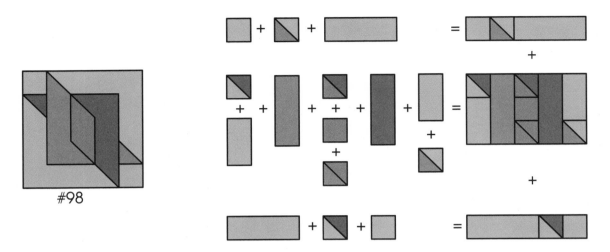

#98

For each block you would need these shapes:

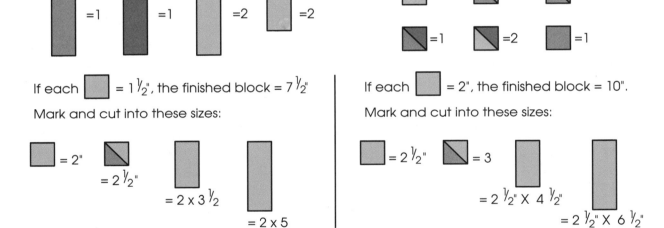

If each ▢ = 1½", the finished block = 7½".

Mark and cut into these sizes:

▢ = 2"
◨ = 2½"
▯ = 2 x 3½
▮ = 2 x 5

If each ▢ = 2", the finished block = 10".

Mark and cut into these sizes:

▢ = 2½"
◨ = 3
▯ = 2½" X 4½"
▮ = 2½" X 6½"

Look at a block carefully to see if it could be pieced more effectively on the diagonal and see in the example below how easily it can be transferred using the grid.. Here is the Rambler:

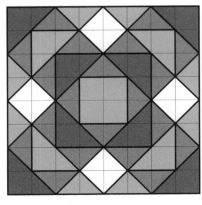

64 squares

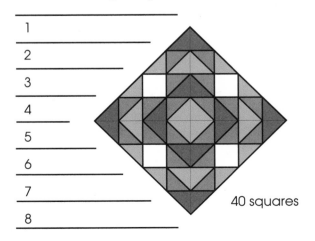

1
2
3
4
5
6
7
8

40 squares

Getting Organized

Stay calm, cool and collected while sewing these pieces into blocks. To keep from getting constantly mixed up, take a few moments to organize yourself at the sewing machine.

On a tray to my left, I place the separate pieces as they will be in the block.

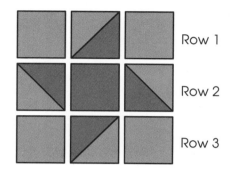

Row 1

Row 2

Row 3

Then I make two stacks of the first two shapes I plan to sew together. (In this case the first two squares in row 1).

} PPM

Now string piece as many of these shapes together as I will need for the whole quilt.

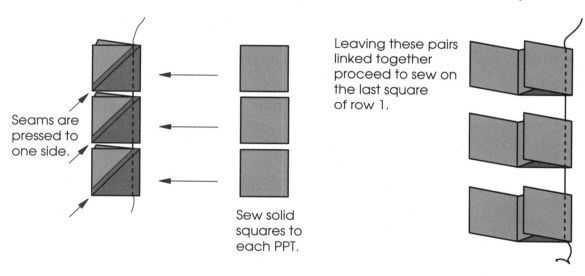

Seams are pressed to one side.

Sew solid squares to each PPT.

Leaving these pairs linked together proceed to sew on the last square of row 1.

Keeping row 1 linked together, set them to one side and make row 2 and row 3 in the same manner.

Now, still keeping separate piles of each row, cut them apart and press seams.

Set row 1 to row 2, one after another. Cut apart and press these seams open.

Add row 3 to each section and there you are! All the blocks are finished!

Helpful Hints for Figuring Yardage

Lots of quilts are made without a particular bed in mind. They wrap the baby on cold days, hang on walls, and are used as throws or just satisfy the quiltmaker's desire to work in plum and gray. These quilts can be whatever size satisfies the design.

If, however, you are making a quilt for a particular bed, measure the bed and start your quilt with those measurements in mind. Consider the things that determine final quilt size like pillow tucks and the desired side drops. For example, some people like to develop a different design to go across the pillows. Because personal taste varies so much on these things, your best bet is to just keep putting the quilt top on the bed as you progress.

If the bed you are planning a specific quilt for is not available to measure, the chart on this page gives some more common mattress surface sizes.

The other two charts are helpful in estimating yardage requirements.

Out of 1 yard of 44" fabric, you can cut this many squares:

Bed	Mattress size
Buggy	15" x 31"
Crib	23" x 46"
Playpen	40" x 40"
Youth	32" x 66"
Studio	30" x 75"
Bunk	38" x 75"
Twin*	39" x 75"
Wide Twin	48" x 75"
Long Twin	39" x 80"
Double*	54" x 75"
Queen*	60" x 80"
King*	78" x 80"
Calif. King	72" x 84"

2" squares	357
2.5"	208
3"	154
3.5"	108
4"	80
4.5"	63
5"	56
5.5"	42
6"	30
6.5"	30
7"	25
7.5"	20
8"	16
8.5"	16
9"	12
9.5"	12
10"	1
10.5"	12
11	9
11.5"-12.5"	6

This chart will help you determine the number of strips or running inches when cutting crosswise on 44" wide fabric:

Strip Size	Strips out of	
	half yard	one yard
1.5"	11	23
2"	8	17
2.5"	7	13
3"	5	11
3.5"	5	10
4"	4	8
4.5"	3	7
5"	3	7
5.5"	3	6
6"	3*	5
7"	2	5
8"	2	4

Running inches out of	
half yard	one yard
462	966
336	714
294	546
210	462
168	336
126	294
84	168

* if careful

Patterns Made Just From Strips

1. Triple Rail Fence

I find the most attractive rail fence quilts are made with five fabrics. Make them in two sets, a dark, medium and light - the light always being the same in both sets.

Special care must be taken when choosing the two mediums. One medium must be closest in value to the dark. The second medium must be closest in value to the light.

This will give you different size fences. Two wide fences and two narrow fences. Now this is my favorite Rail Fence quilt. I think that it has more activity and excitement. It is an easy way to get a more interesting design with no more effort.

There are a few things that I'm stubborn about. It's okay if you make the Rail Fence another way - just don't say you learned it from me!

My favorite size strips for this quilt are 2" cut (1 ½" finished). In the diagram shown, the strip can be any width you want. They must be the same width in the same quilt.

To make a quilt 72" x 81" you would need (theoretically pure - that means using every inch): 1 ¼ yards of colors 1, 2, 3 and 4
            2 ½ yards of color 5
If you want to be safe, buy a little more or add frames (borders).

Measure and mark your fabric into 2" strips. Cut strips. Divide strips into 2 groups as shown below and sew together. Iron seams toward the darker side.

Color 1   Color 2

Color 3   Color 4

Color 5

Set #1

Set #2

Triple Rail Fence, continued

After sewing your set of 3 strips together, measure side to side (raw edge to raw edge). This is your PPM. Cut sections apart equal to this measurement.

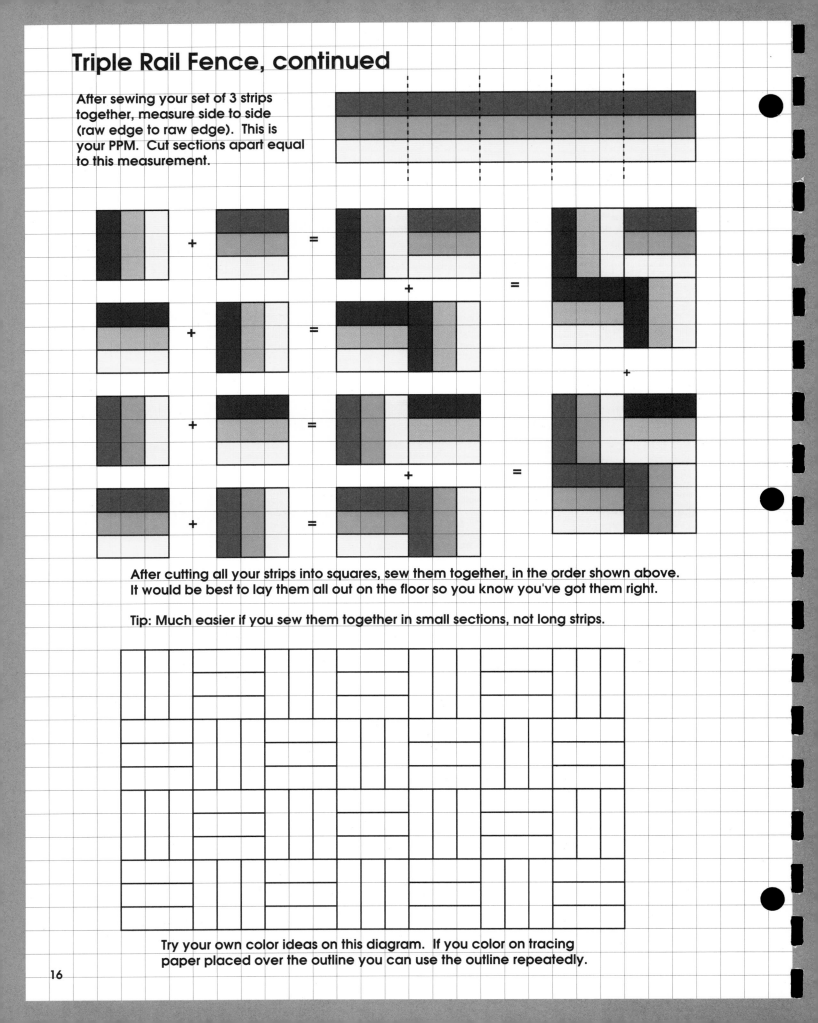

After cutting all your strips into squares, sew them together, in the order shown above. It would be best to lay them all out on the floor so you know you've got them right.

Tip: Much easier if you sew them together in small sections, not long strips.

Try your own color ideas on this diagram. If you color on tracing paper placed over the outline you can use the outline repeatedly.

2. Amish Shadow

This quilt is traditionally made with bright, bold stripes, set off by a solid black "shadow".

The traditional setting for the blocks is shown below, but feel free to come up with your own pattern. These blocks can be arranged to create an endless variety of designs. Have fun!

To make this quilt top, you will need: 1/4 yard of seven solid fabrics, 45" wide.
1 1/2 yards black, 45" wide.

Measure and mark the colored fabrics into 1 1/2" strips. Cut and divide into groups of five strips. Mix your colors to create different combinations of colors. Sew the strips together. Iron seams to one side.

Using a template, mark your triangle on the sewn strips. Cut. You will get seven triangles from each set of strips.

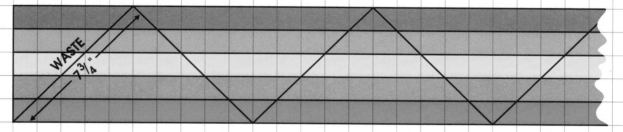

You will have to experiment to find your size square. Start with a 7 3/4" square folded in half. You will see immediately whether or not you will need a smaller or larger square.

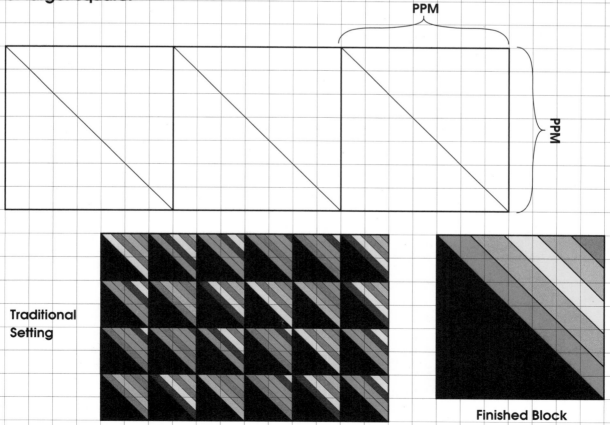

Traditional Setting

Finished Block

Amish Shadow, continued

For a quilt that is 6 x 8 (48 blocks), about 41" x 55",
you will need to cut a total of 35 strips measuring
1½" (not necessarily an equal number of each
color, and I suggest only 1 or 2 strips of your
lightest color.)

You will need 1½ yards of solid black, cut as shown:

Here are some variations
of the Amish Shadow.
Experiment with your
blocks. The variations
are endless.

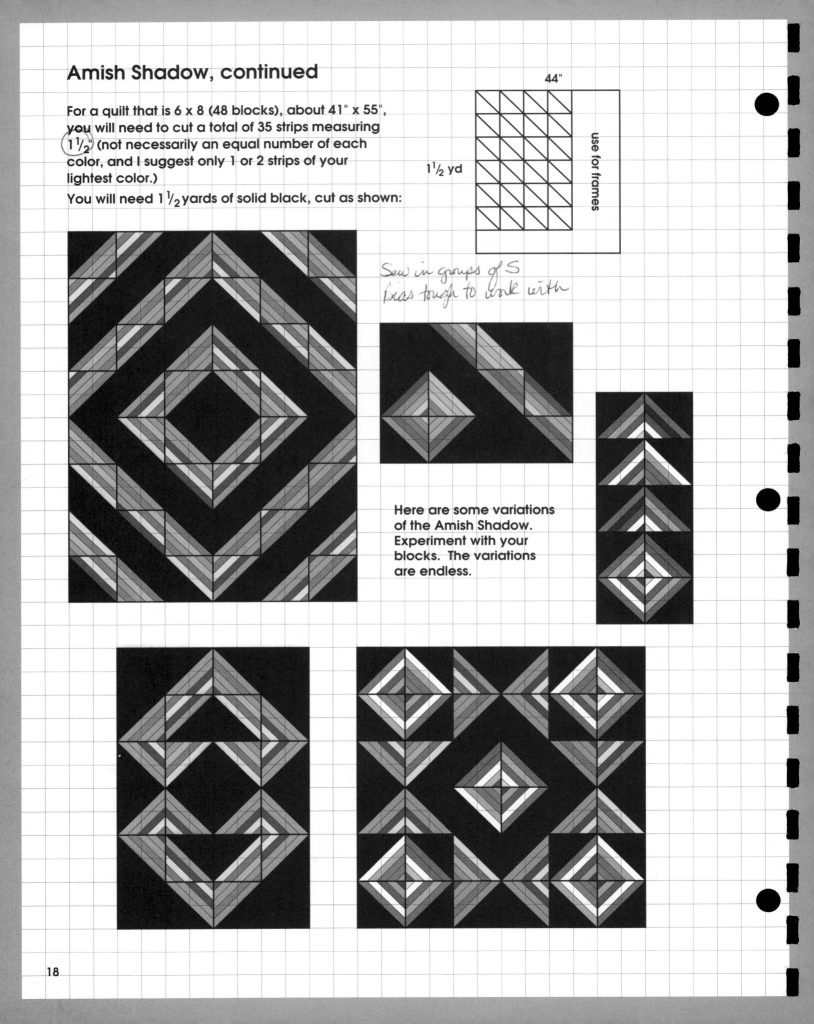

44"

1½ yd

use for frames

Sew in groups of 5
Bias tough to work with

3. Log Cabin

Log Cabin is probably the single most popular quilt made from strips. It is so popular because it's almost magic. As long as you can tell dark material from light material, you can hardly go wrong.

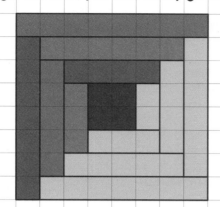

The Log Cabin block is worked from a center square out. Strips are added to one side at a time, rotating the square after each addition. There are no "rules" as to the number of strips, their width or size of the finished square in relationship to the center square.

My favorite size for a double bed or larger is a 2" cut square and three $1\frac{1}{2}$" cut strips on each side of the square. The block is about 8" finished.

Learn the technique and you'll love it forever!

Traditional Log Cabin Block

Start with the center square and your first light strip, right sides together. Sew your presser foot seam allowance down one side.

center

light strip

← cut

Cut off the strip even with the center square. Open the first strip out. Lay the second light strip across the first strip and the square, right sides together. Stitch down the side (your presser foot seam allowance from the edge), then cut the strip even with the square.

light strip

cut

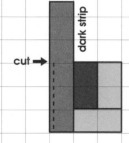

dark strip

cut →

The third strip is your first dark strip. Proceed in the same way around the center square. Always rotate in the same direction. Keep adding strips until you get the desired size square.

cut

dark strip

light strip next

I think these blocks are always more charming if they have a "scrap" look. When you really get hooked on quilting, you'll probably keep two boxes like I do. One has light strips and the other, dark strips.

Since the more popular width is $1\frac{1}{2}$", you could cut up suitable leftover fabrics from other projects into $1\frac{1}{2}$" strips (any length) and store them in the appropriate box. It's perfect for a Sunday afternoon when you want to do something, but you don't want to think too much.

Personally, I'm into $1\frac{1}{4}$" strips.

Log Cabin, continued

The Log Cabin block doesn't even demand "pretty" fabrics - absolutely anything works. Traditionally, the center block was red to signify the chimney. If you are doing a pure scrap quilt, a shade of red is still a good choice. Even some pioneer ladies were maverick enough to use another color, so don't feel bound to red. If you are selecting fabrics with a color scheme in mind (mostly blues and greens, for example), select the center square last, like an accent, instead of first when it would set the tone of the entire quilt.

If you don't have an automatic scrap pile, I suggest this way for selecting fabric. Very simple - buy 10 half yard pieces (about five yards total) of dark fabrics. Then select 10 half yard pieces of light fabric. Good variety in light tones seems more difficult to find. If necessary, you may buy five yards of just one fabric for the light half. Buy a half yard for the centers. If there is a fabric you think you want to make borders, buy it when you see it!

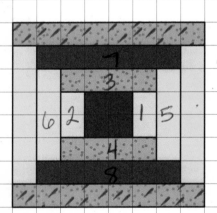

Courthouse Steps

Again, this starts with a center, but the strips are sewn on one pair of opposite sides first, then the other.

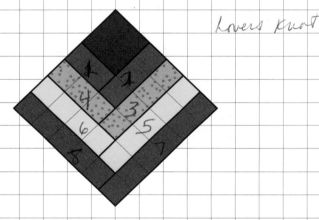

Lovers Knot

Chevron Log Cabin

The square is moved to the corner and strips are added to two sides only. Typically, each fabric is repeated twice to emphasize chevron design and blocks are set together diagonally with window-paning that matches the center blocks.

These are only two variations. Current literature abounds with scenic Log Cabin designs, Log Cabin techniques with various center shapes and varying strip widths

These are some of the more commonly used Log Cabin sets. Try some of these sets with the Amish Shadow.

Barn Raising

Sunshine and Shadows

Square with Ring Around

A Beautiful Frame

Flying Geese

When piecing these sections, you'll need a block that is all dark, no lights.

100 Blocks

4 center blocks
32 middle blocks
64 outer blocks

4. Double Irish Chain

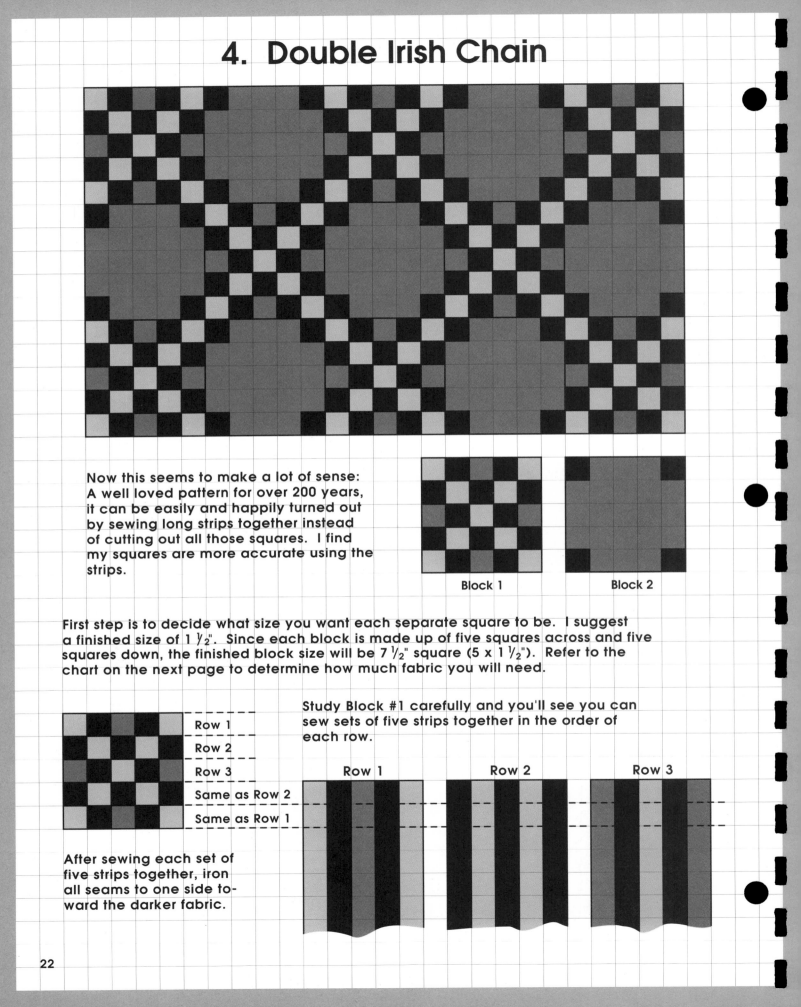

Now this seems to make a lot of sense:
A well loved pattern for over 200 years,
it can be easily and happily turned out
by sewing long strips together instead
of cutting out all those squares. I find
my squares are more accurate using the
strips.

Block 1   Block 2

First step is to decide what size you want each separate square to be. I suggest
a finished size of 1 $\frac{1}{2}$". Since each block is made up of five squares across and five
squares down, the finished block size will be 7 $\frac{1}{2}$" square (5 x 1 $\frac{1}{2}$"). Refer to the
chart on the next page to determine how much fabric you will need.

Row 1
Row 2
Row 3
Same as Row 2
Same as Row 1

Study Block #1 carefully and you'll see you can
sew sets of five strips together in the order of
each row.

Row 1   Row 2   Row 3

After sewing each set of
five strips together, iron
all seams to one side to-
ward the darker fabric.

22

How To Piece Block 2 If You Are Machine Quilting

PPM

Your Personal
Private Block 1

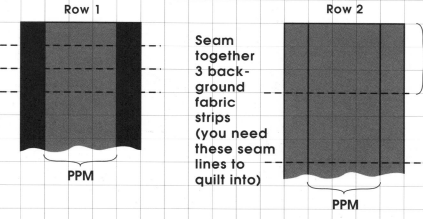

Row 1

Row 2

same as Row 1

Turn your very
own Block 1
over and measure
your 3 squares
worth, raw edge
to raw edge.
This will be your
PPM.

Row 1

Row 2

PPM

PPM

Seam
together
3 back-
ground
fabric
strips
(you need
these seam
lines to
quilt into)

PPM

PPM

A balanced quilt design demands an odd number of squares in each direction.

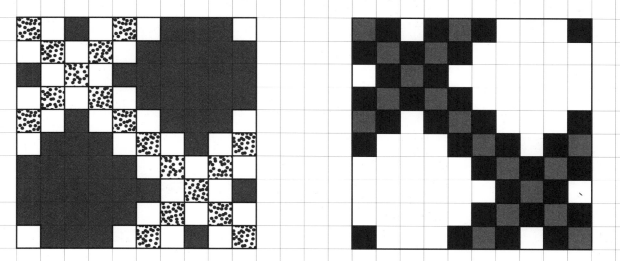

Yardage for Double Irish Chain

The following measurements are based on $1\frac{1}{2}$" finished square
which gives you about a $7\frac{1}{2}$" finished block.

Number of blocks across and down	Approximate Size	Camel	Black	Rust
5 x 7	$37\frac{1}{2}$ x $52\frac{1}{2}$	$\frac{3}{4}$	1	$1\frac{1}{4}$
7 x 9	$52\frac{1}{2}$ x $67\frac{1}{2}$	$1\frac{1}{2}$	2	$2\frac{1}{2}$
9 x 11	$67\frac{1}{2}$ x $82\frac{1}{2}$	$2\frac{1}{4}$	3	$3\frac{3}{4}$
11 x 13	$82\frac{1}{2}$ x $97\frac{1}{2}$	3	4	5

5. Mandevilla

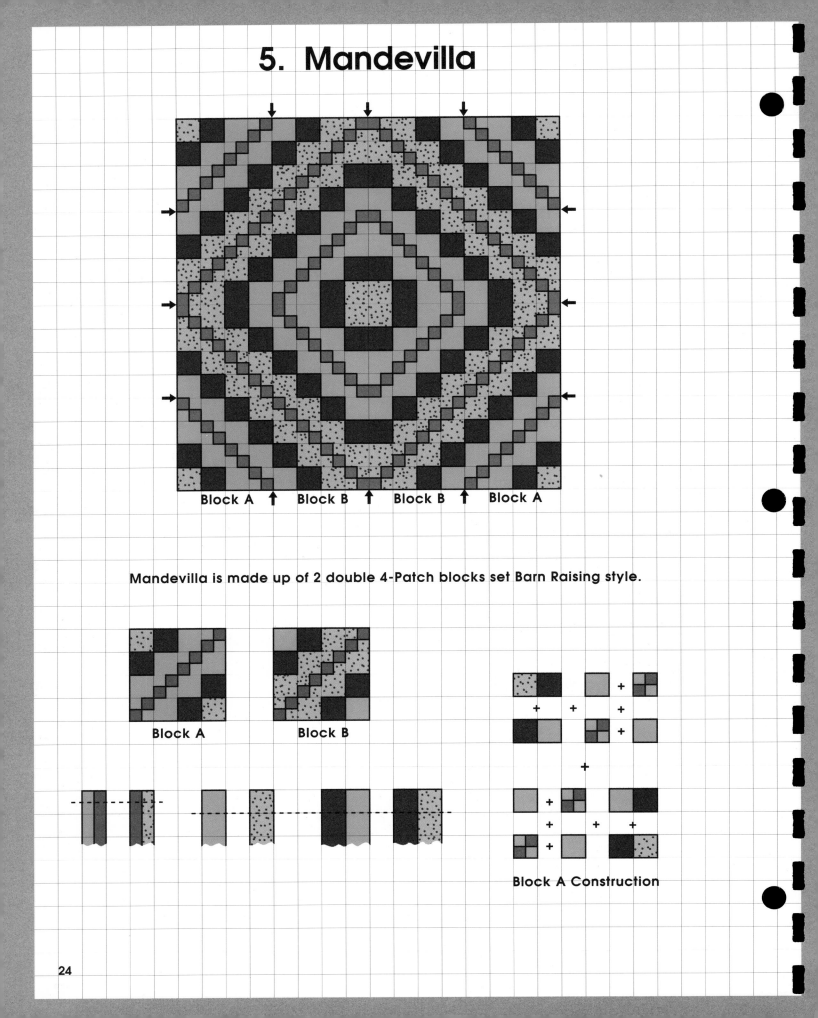

Block A   ↑   Block B   ↑   Block B   ↑   Block A

Mandevilla is made up of 2 double 4-Patch blocks set Barn Raising style.

Block A

Block B

Block A Construction

Secrets No One Ever Told You

Secrets No One Ever Told You

1. The Connecting Block

Everyone has seen quilts where a patchwork block is set together with an alternate plain block. When you do this, an empty square of solid fabric demands lots of quilting. If the empty square is a print, if often looks like you got lazy and tried to make two quilts from one set of squares.

One of the best kept secrets is the use of a simple connecting block or what I often call a connector. Connectors are simple pieced squares not generally recognized as a patchwork pattern. They would look something like these:

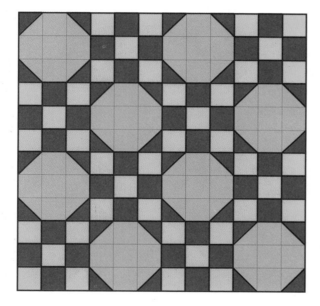

...and are the same size as your finished block. Use it instead of a plain alternating block and suddenly your quilt takes on a finished over-all look.

Here are some 9-patch variations.

 +

These are the same block, but see how different they look.

 +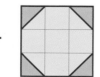

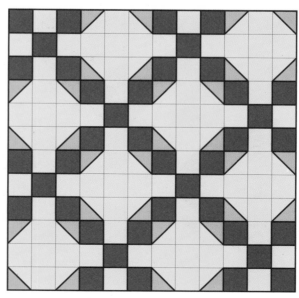

Connecting Block, continued

King's Crown picks up a wonderful star as a secondary design:

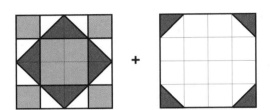 +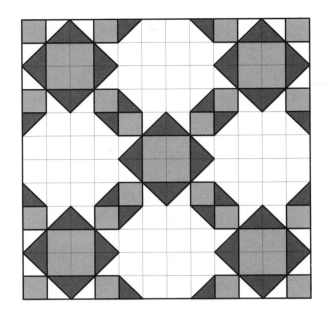

Look what the connector block does for the Northwind.

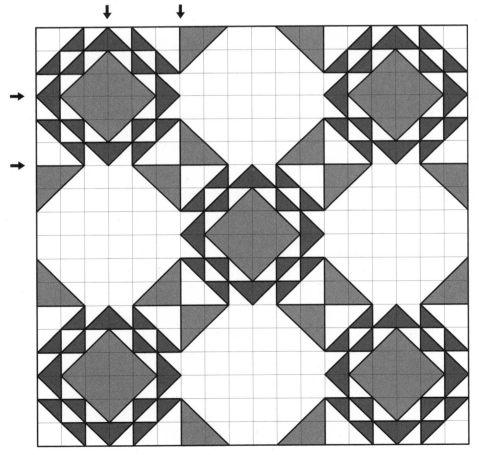

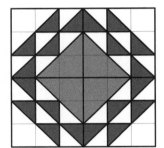

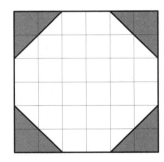

This makes a pretty quilt with a few actual blocks and nice empty spaces for quilting.

2. Combining Squares

Combining Squares is the next step in the progression. It is actually combining different recognized quilt patterns. This is usually done in an alternating pattern, but certainly shouldn't be confined to that. Linked Stars, #83, page 48 and World Without End, #78, page 45 are both excellent examples. If you want to play with developing designs using two patterns, don't forget how helpful it is to use the copy machine to get enough repeats.

A variation of Combining Squares is putting positive and negative versions of the same design together. Double T, #162, page 106 and the positive /negative version of Gentleman's Fancy, page 101 are both examples.

3. Floating

Windowpaning or sashing is the name for the border or frame of fabric that goes around a single quilt block. (If a block develops an exciting secondary pattern, I don't recommend windowpaning.)

The secret I want to share is a very special kind of windowpaning I call floating. Quite simply, floating just means a strip of the background fabric around a block. When you are using blocks that don't make great secondary designs like the Little Bow, English Ivy, some baskets, trees, or other recognizable shapes, a small windowpaning border of the background fabric makes that design float! So when you don't want the blocks to intermingle into a secondary pattern and you do want them to stand out, float them. Size of the floating strip is not crucial. You may want to add contrasting windowpaning, but this subtle floater strip is very important. It can be especially important in single block designs like pillows and purses. The floater strip keeps the design from bleeding off the edge or mingling with a border.

The Little Ribbon Bow, #229, page 65 and Double Links, #189, page 60 need to float no matter how you use them.

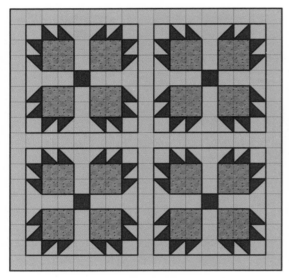

English Ivy -
Floating keeps
these "leaves"
from touching.

Bear's Paw with a border
Dark lines define block

4. Breaking Into the Border

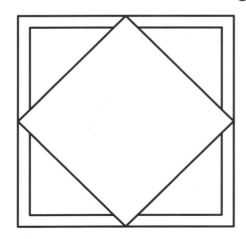

Borders don't have to be straight. Breaking into them with the central design is one of the easiest ways to give an "uptown look" to an ordinary quilt. This is most easily done when you're working with a diagonal set. The corners of the diagonal just dip into the borders.

5. What to Look for in Working Up a Pattern

Are you going crazy trying to find that great next little pattern to work up?

As you're going through pages and pages of little designs there is a neat trick about picking out the most exciting ones to play with.

As you look at a block, listen for certain little bells to ring.

 1st Bell: Is there a diagonal line through the block that your eye can see?

A Log Cabin block has a diagonal line:

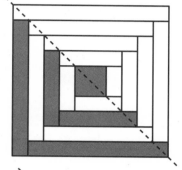

....and Wedding March

So does the simple 3-patch sailboat:

All of the "Road" blocks have the diagonal lines.
All of these blocks will twist around and make great secondary designs.

2nd Bell: Are there at least two different corners?

The block Aircraft has unbalanced opposite corners:

The simple Sailboat and Northwind do also:

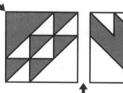

We can **make** the Wedding March have unbalanced corners. We want to make it have a second bell because it's such an easy little block to make with the easy strips and 9-Patch center.

Your eyes will always see a nice little balanced, finished looking block. All the Tree Blocks, the Baskets, English Ivy, Autumn Leaf, and Double Link are very nice, but they don't make the unusual, exciting secondary designs. Those funny, odd-looking, unbalanced blocks that are not as frequently chosen are terrific to work with. So when looking at quilt blocks, **listen** for two bells.

Working Up a Pattern, continued

The best solution I've found to play with all these funny little blocks and keep your sanity: On a sheet of graph paper draw 4 blocks each of several different patterns and then go to your local copy machine and have several copies run off. Now you've got several of each little block to cut apart and play with by twisting this way and that. You do realize you'll become a late night movie buff!

For an even more challenging step, draw only the lines of the block (no fill-in). After you've twisted them around and pasted them down then do some fill -in, as we did with Joseph's Coat, page 103.

6. Setting a Design "On Point"

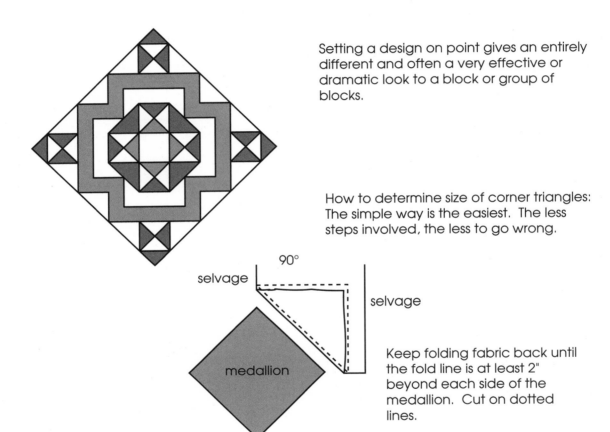

Setting a design on point gives an entirely different and often a very effective or dramatic look to a block or group of blocks.

How to determine size of corner triangles: The simple way is the easiest. The less steps involved, the less to go wrong.

Keep folding fabric back until the fold line is at least 2" beyond each side of the medallion. Cut on dotted lines.

Why cut so big?

1. If the side triangles end up too small, the next seam will knock the tip of the square off and ruin the center design.

2. You may decide you want the medallion "embedded" in the background fabric and you will need the extra for that effect.

3. Just because it's easy to cut off the excess, but you can't glue fabric on when it's too small.

Don't cut any excess fabric until your next straight border is attached.

7. Diagonal Sets

When lots of small squares are set "on point" in the same design, we call it a diagonal set. I like diagonal sets so much I say "when in doubt, put it on the diagonal". The first and most important secret about diagonal sets is how to cut those half blocks for the sides.

To determine the size of the square that you cut into quarters, add a minimum of 3" to the diagonal measurement of the finished square (see chart on Page 33).

How To Cut Your Half Blocks

In order to maintain straight grain on the edges of the corner pieces, the four corner blocks will be squares cut in half, not fourths. Cut two squares at least 2" larger than the measurement of the finished block. Cut in half diagonally for the corners.

Step 1:
Measure across the diagonal of the block.

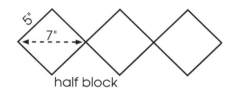

half block

Step 2:
Make a square 3" - 4" larger than diagonal measurement (7" + 3" = 10").

Step 3:
Cut into quarters. This way all the edges will be on the straight of the fabric. The half blocks will be larger than you need, but that's good - you can always trim down afterwards.

Here's what your top will look like, with the larger half blocks:

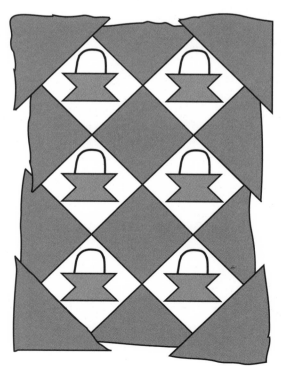

If this is the whole of your quilt top, leave it alone, and plan on bringing the back of the quilt to the front. You will have plenty of fabric on the front to "bite" into.

If you want to add a border around this it's very easy to just lay your strip as far in from the edge as needed to achieve the proper seam line. Quite often your quilt top has gotten "out of line" by now and this is a great time to straighten it up. If trimming, make sure you leave necessary seam allowances.

The second secret about diagonal sets and a hard and fast rule is to lay the blocks out with the half blocks **before** you start sewing them together. Now pick up the diagonal rows with the half blocks on each end, one row at a time, and sew each row together. Now you can sew the completed rows together.

Diagonal Sets, continued

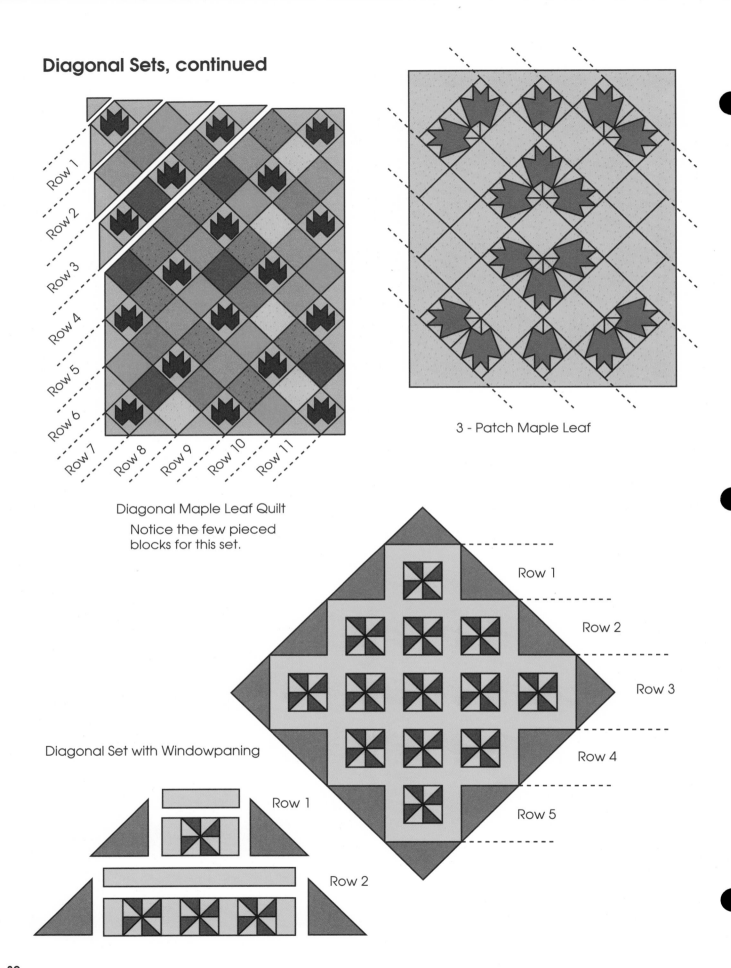

Row 1
Row 2
Row 3
Row 4
Row 5
Row 6
Row 7 Row 8 Row 9 Row 10 Row 11

Diagonal Maple Leaf Quilt
Notice the few pieced
blocks for this set.

3 - Patch Maple Leaf

Diagonal Set with Windowpaning

Row 1
Row 2
Row 3
Row 4
Row 5

Row 1
Row 2

Measuring Diagonal Sets

Remember how to find the hypotenuse of a triangle? $a^2 + b^2 = c^2$

Square	Diagonal	Square	Diagonal
1.5"	2.12"	11	15.6
2	2.8	12	17
3	4.24	13	18.38
4	5.65	14	19.8
5	7. +	15	21.21
6	8.48	16	22.6
7	9.9	17	24
8	11.31	18	25.4
9	12.73	20	28.28
10	14.14		

That's the mathematical way to find the diagonal measurement for the square abc. Just in case you don't remember, this handy chart gives you the diagonal measurement of these squares.

Of course you'll round these measurements off in either direction.

How to Figure the Number of Blocks Needed for a Diagonal Set

When quilt squares are set together "square with the world", it's easy to know how many 10" blocks are needed for a quilt 80" x 100" with no borders. It's not so easy with a diagonal set.

If you have a 10" block the diagonal is just over 14". That 80" x 100" quilt would hold five plus blocks across and seven plus blocks down - but wait, that's only on what we call the outside row. The "inside rows" need to be calculated, too. Often the inside rows are a contrasting fabric design so it is important to know exactly how many of each block to make or cut.

For example,
on this quilt you will need:

20 block #1

12 block #2

14 half blocks for the side and
 4 corners

Diagonal Sets, continued

This diagram should be helpful for your own figuring.

Quilt size outside row	# of blocks outside row	# of blocks inside row	# of total blocks	# of half blocks
4 x 6	24 +	15 =	39	16
5 x 5	25 +	16 =	41	16
6 x 6	36 +	25 =	61	20
6 x 8	48 +	35 =	83	24
7 x 7	49 +	36 =	85	24
8 x 9	80 +	63 =	143	32
10 x 10	100 +	81 =	181	36
10 x 12	120 +	99 =	219	40

There are always four corners.

About these "patches"...

In the following chapter you will be introduced to "the patches". Each of them will be numbered with its name or a blank.

Now, I have to say that I'm not really hung up on the names of quilts. First of all, there are lots of different names for different patterns, and secondly, I like to name some of my own quilts. It would be like having your children already named when they are born. However, it seems that quilt book readers expect to find names with each quilt block. So, this is what I've done. On those squares that carry names, these are the names that I have learned to identify with that particular design over the years.

If I have never learned a name, or perhaps a square is a variation or a "doodle", I have identified it with a number for reference only. You may want to name some of these squares yourself.

I have to admit, I will be disappointed if at some quilt show in the next few years I don't see a quilt titled "No. 39, Revisited", or "No. 4, In Mirror Image". That lets me know that the blocks in this book were in fact your inspiration.

The Three Little Patches

The Mock Log Cabin

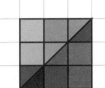

1. Mock Log Cabin

Barn Raising

My favorite of all the scrap quilt patterns! This charming little block should be used just as you would use a Log Cabin block.

On the right are sketched a Barn Raising set and a Straight Furrows set. Use any of your favorite Log Cabin sets.

To be effective, you must have lights in your darks and vice versa.

Columbus, Ohio

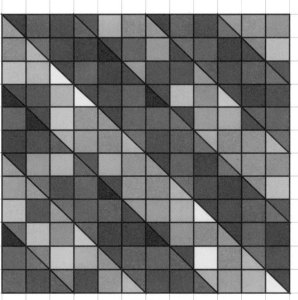

Straight Furrows

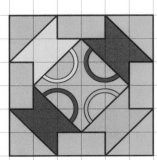

2. 13¢ Postage Stamp

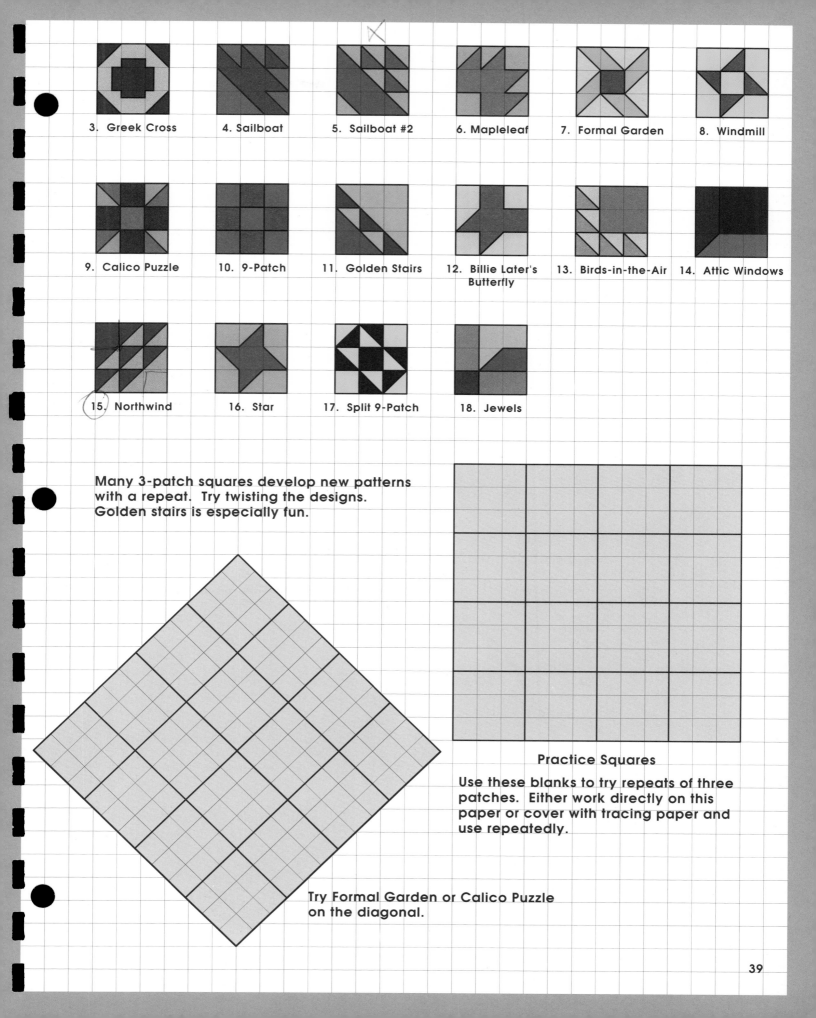

3. Greek Cross 　　4. Sailboat 　　5. Sailboat #2 　　6. Mapleleaf 　　7. Formal Garden 　　8. Windmill

9. Calico Puzzle 　　10. 9-Patch 　　11. Golden Stairs 　　12. Billie Later's Butterfly 　　13. Birds-in-the-Air 　　14. Attic Windows

15. Northwind 　　16. Star 　　17. Split 9-Patch 　　18. Jewels

Many 3-patch squares develop new patterns with a repeat. Try twisting the designs. Golden stairs is especially fun.

Practice Squares

Use these blanks to try repeats of three patches. Either work directly on this paper or cover with tracing paper and use repeatedly.

Try Formal Garden or Calico Puzzle on the diagonal.

40

Four Patch

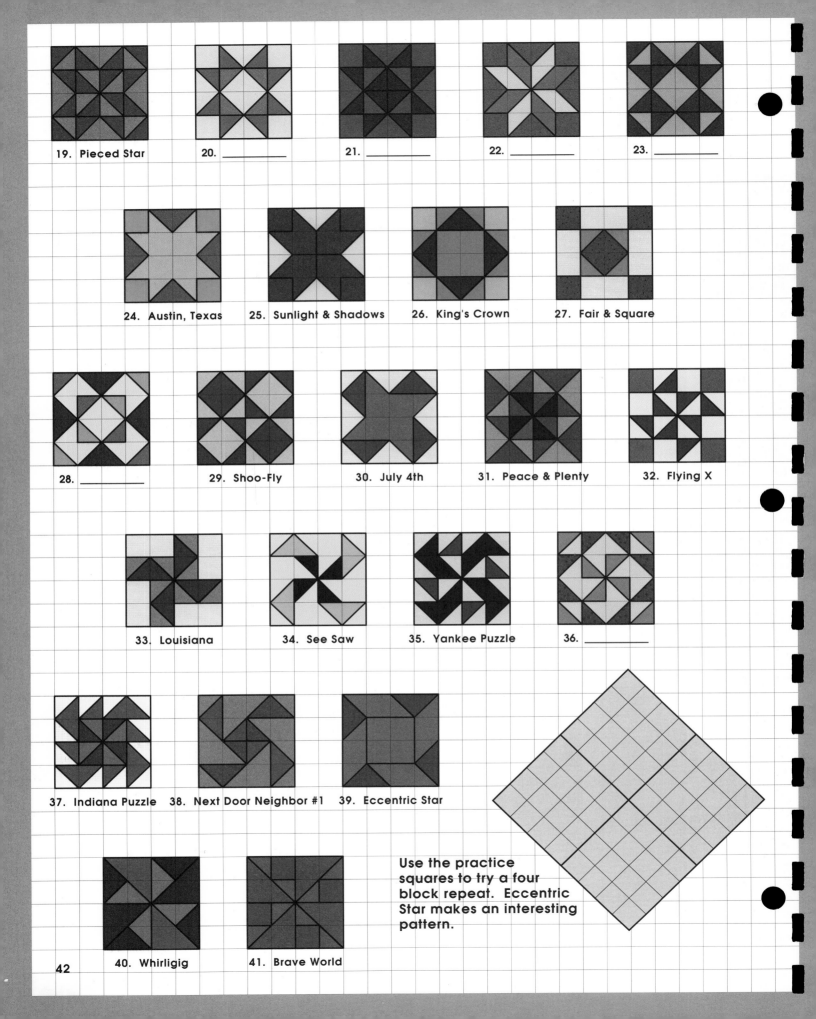

19. **Pieced Star**

20. _____

21. _____

22. _____

23. _____

24. **Austin, Texas**

25. **Sunlight & Shadows**

26. **King's Crown**

27. **Fair & Square**

28. _____

29. **Shoo-Fly**

30. **July 4th**

31. **Peace & Plenty**

32. **Flying X**

33. **Louisiana**

34. **See Saw**

35. **Yankee Puzzle**

36. _____

37. **Indiana Puzzle**

38. **Next Door Neighbor #1**

39. **Eccentric Star**

Use the practice squares to try a four block repeat. Eccentric Star makes an interesting pattern.

40. **Whirligig**

41. **Brave World**

42

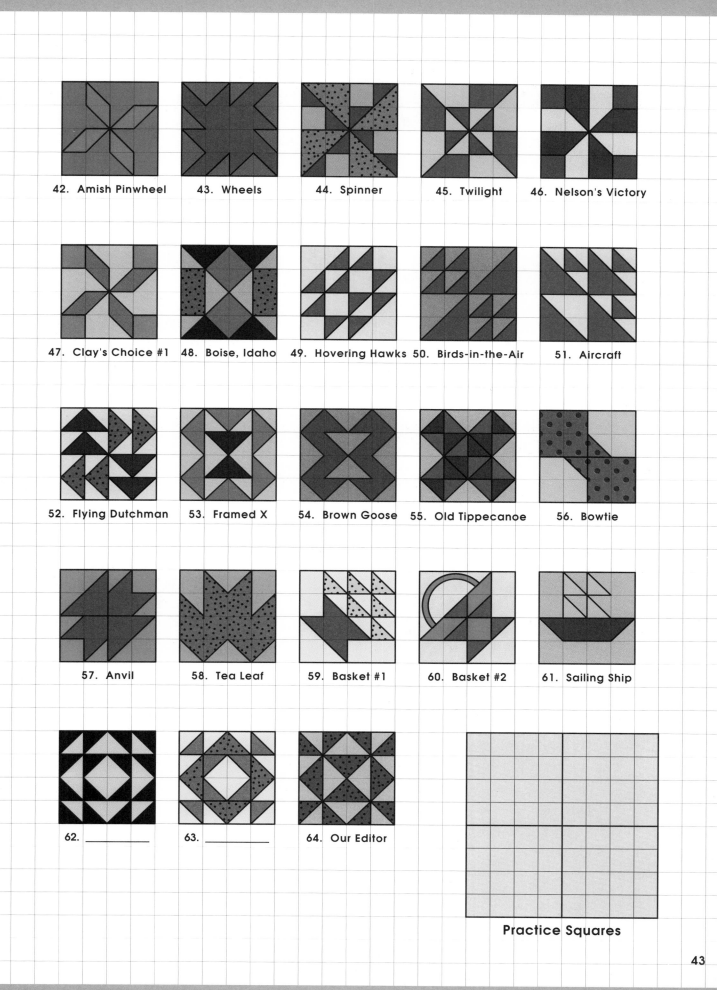

42. Amish Pinwheel

43. Wheels

44. Spinner

45. Twilight

46. Nelson's Victory

47. Clay's Choice #1

48. Boise, Idaho

49. Hovering Hawks

50. Birds-in-the-Air

51. Aircraft

52. Flying Dutchman

53. Framed X

54. Brown Goose

55. Old Tippecanoe

56. Bowtie

57. Anvil

58. Tea Leaf

59. Basket #1

60. Basket #2

61. Sailing Ship

62. _____

63. _____

64. Our Editor

Practice Squares

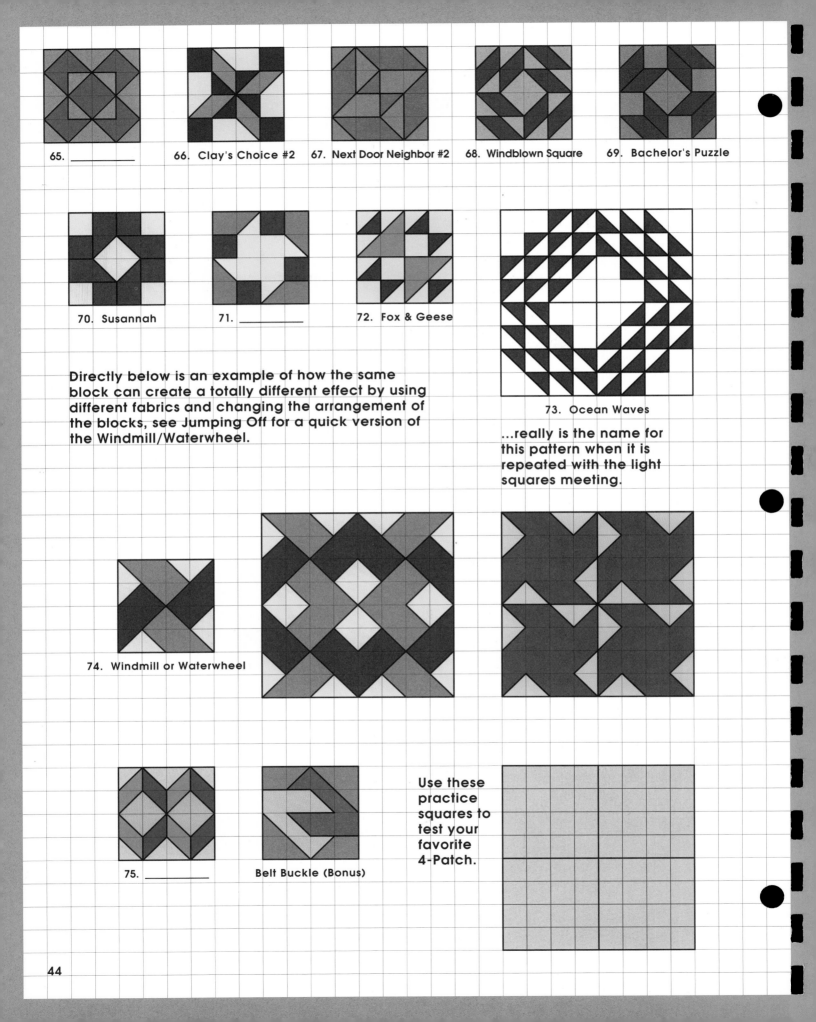

65. _____

66. Clay's Choice #2

67. Next Door Neighbor #2

68. Windblown Square

69. Bachelor's Puzzle

70. Susannah

71. _____

72. Fox & Geese

73. Ocean Waves

Directly below is an example of how the same block can create a totally different effect by using different fabrics and changing the arrangement of the blocks, see Jumping Off for a quick version of the Windmill/Waterwheel.

...really is the name for this pattern when it is repeated with the light squares meeting.

74. Windmill or Waterwheel

75. _____

Belt Buckle (Bonus)

Use these practice squares to test your favorite 4-Patch.

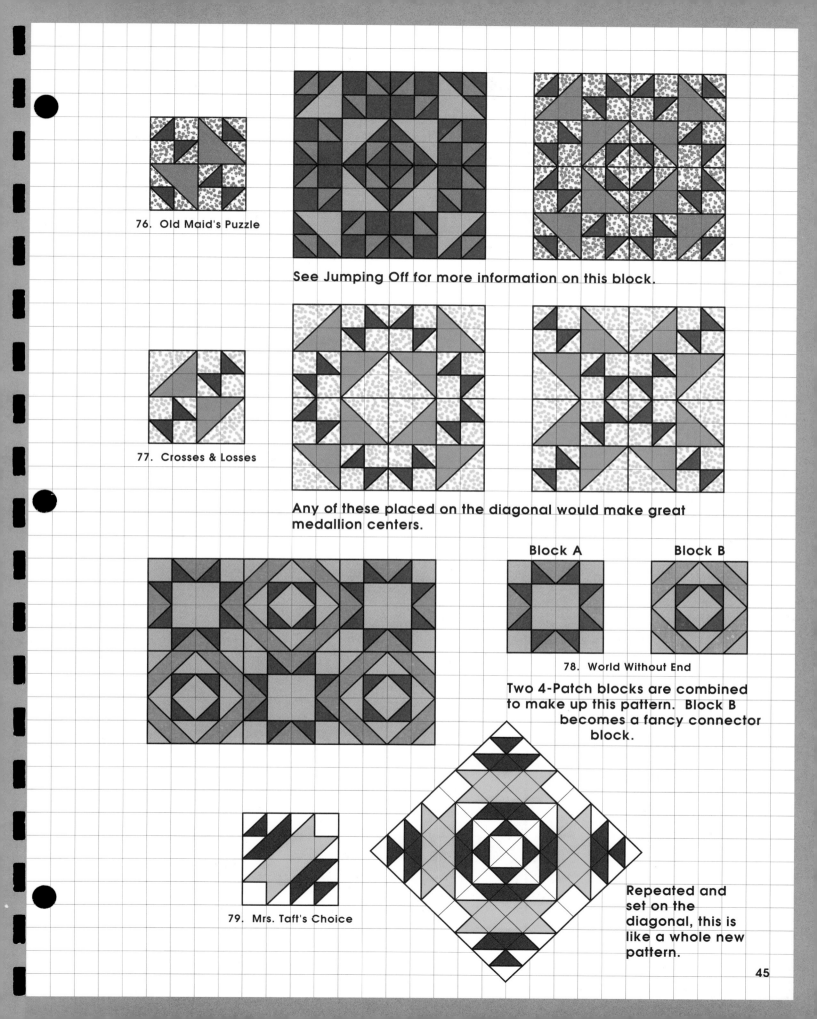

76. Old Maid's Puzzle

See Jumping Off for more information on this block.

77. Crosses & Losses

Any of these placed on the diagonal would make great medallion centers.

Block A

Block B

78. World Without End

Two 4-Patch blocks are combined to make up this pattern. Block B becomes a fancy connector block.

79. Mrs. Taft's Choice

Repeated and set on the diagonal, this is like a whole new pattern.

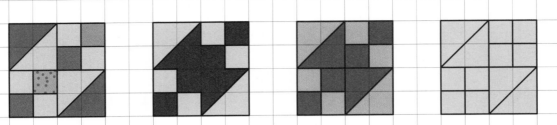

Notice this is a two bell block!!

Study these blocks carefully. Do you see that they are the same basic 4-Patch block? Below and on the following page we have illustrated three different patterns that are made up of this one basic block. Different color placement and arrangement of the block produce these different variations. We have left one block blank for you to fill in. Experiment with this block. The variations are endless.

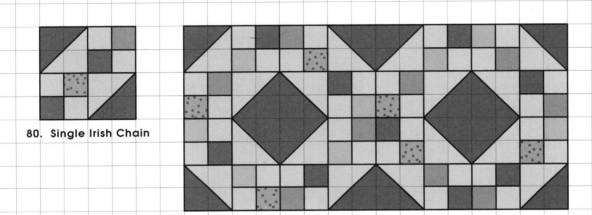

80. Single Irish Chain

This is the fastest of the scrap quilts. Make all your triangles at the very beginning, then you can take your time making the little 4-Patches. I suggest you put some of the fabric that makes the large squares away in a safe place in case you want to add borders later.

81. Buckeye Beauty

Jacob's Ladder - Variation

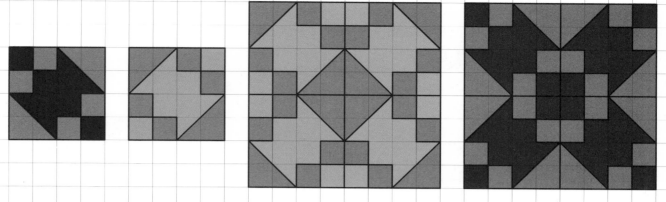

This quilt is made up of nine blocks that are made up of four blocks of Buckeye Beauty.

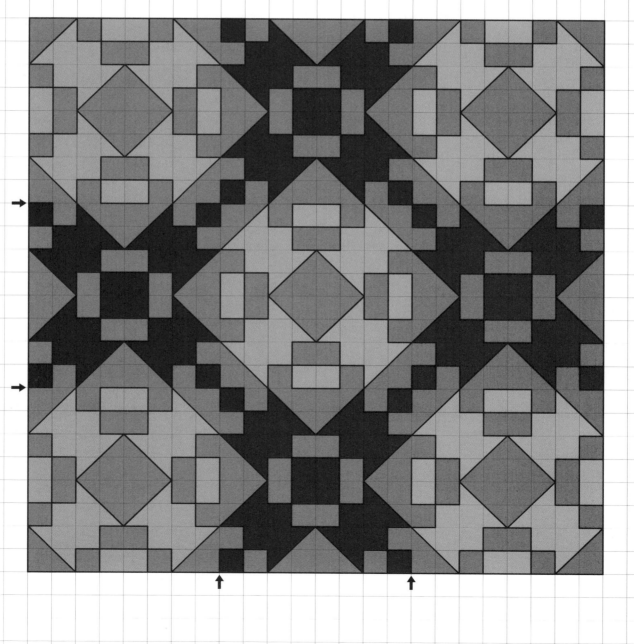

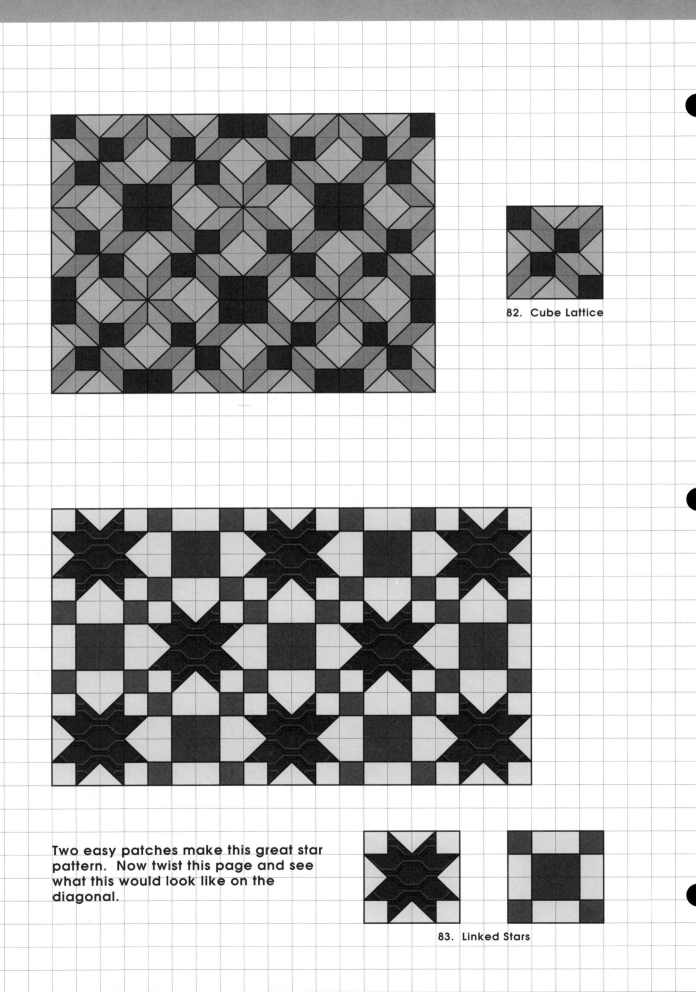

82. Cube Lattice

Two easy patches make this great star pattern. Now twist this page and see what this would look like on the diagonal.

83. Linked Stars

48

Five
Patch

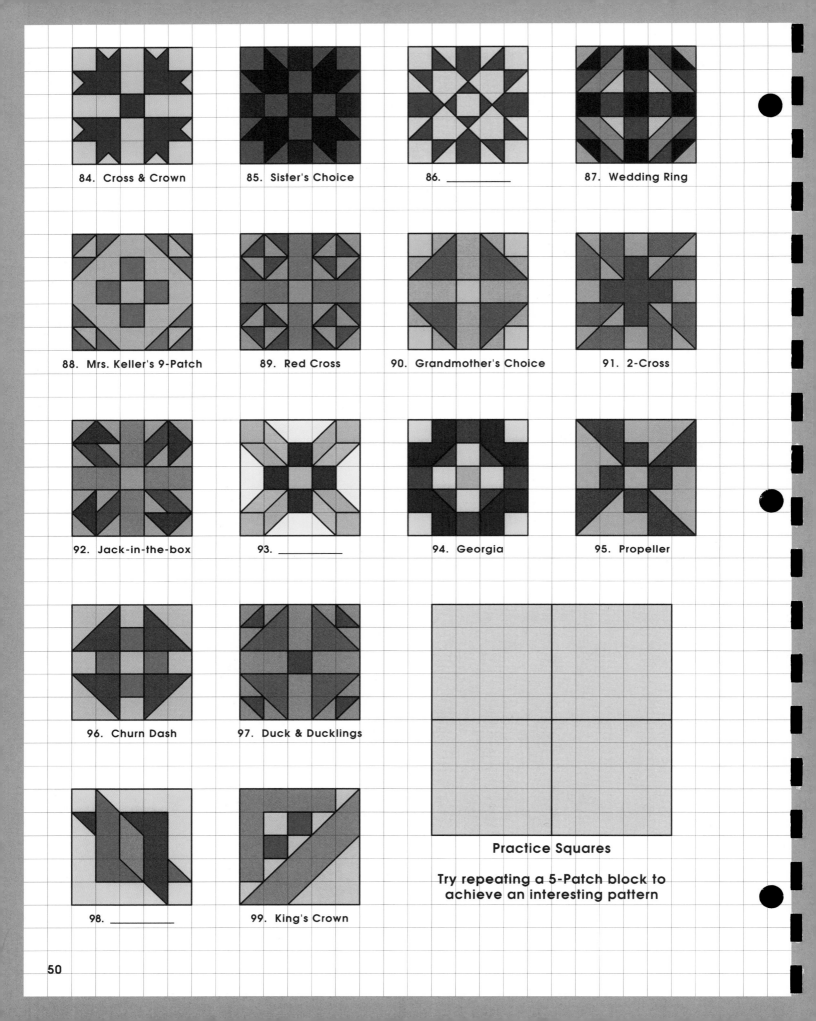

84. Cross & Crown

85. Sister's Choice

86. _____

87. Wedding Ring

88. Mrs. Keller's 9-Patch

89. Red Cross

90. Grandmother's Choice

91. 2-Cross

92. Jack-in-the-box

93. _____

94. Georgia

95. Propeller

96. Churn Dash

97. Duck & Ducklings

Practice Squares

Try repeating a 5-Patch block to achieve an interesting pattern

98. _____

99. King's Crown

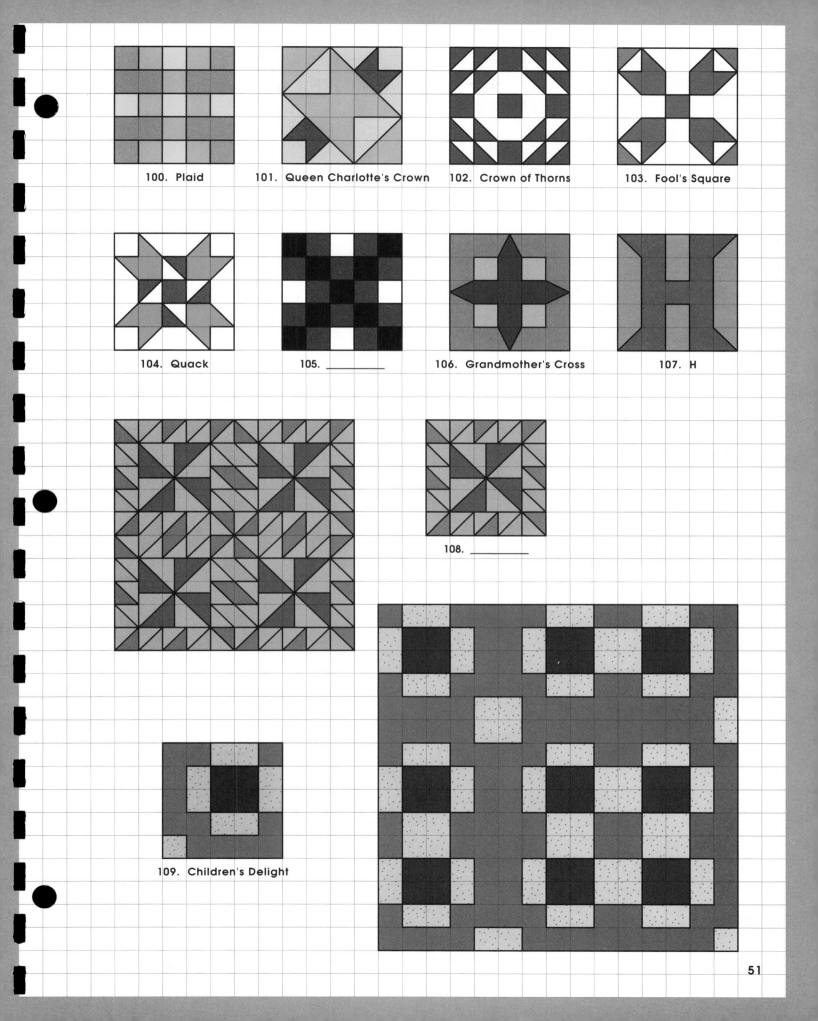

100. Plaid

101. Queen Charlotte's Crown

102. Crown of Thorns

103. Fool's Square

104. Quack

105. _____

106. Grandmother's Cross

107. H

108. _____

109. Children's Delight

51

110. Double Sawtooth

111. Basket

112. Flower Pot

113. Sawtooth

114. Grape Basket

115. Cake Stand

116. Basket of Scraps

117. Tree

118. Lady of the Lake

119. _____

120. _____

52

Six Patch

121. Lost Ship

122. Corn & Beans

123. _____

124. _____

125. Winged Square

126. Indian Plume

127. Strawberry Basket

128. Combination Star

129. Snowball

130. _____

131. _____

132. Illinois

The three designs above were all made using blocks of this little 3-Patch.

Notice - another two bell block!

54

133. Arkansas Traveler

134. Rolling Stone #1

135. Rolling Stone #2

136. Prairie Queen

137. Dumbbell

138. Gentleman's Fancy

139. Aunt Eliza's Star

140. Ohio Star

141. _____

142. _____

Notice how in one square, the corners seem anchored. When repeated, the corners become the major design, and the centers float.

55

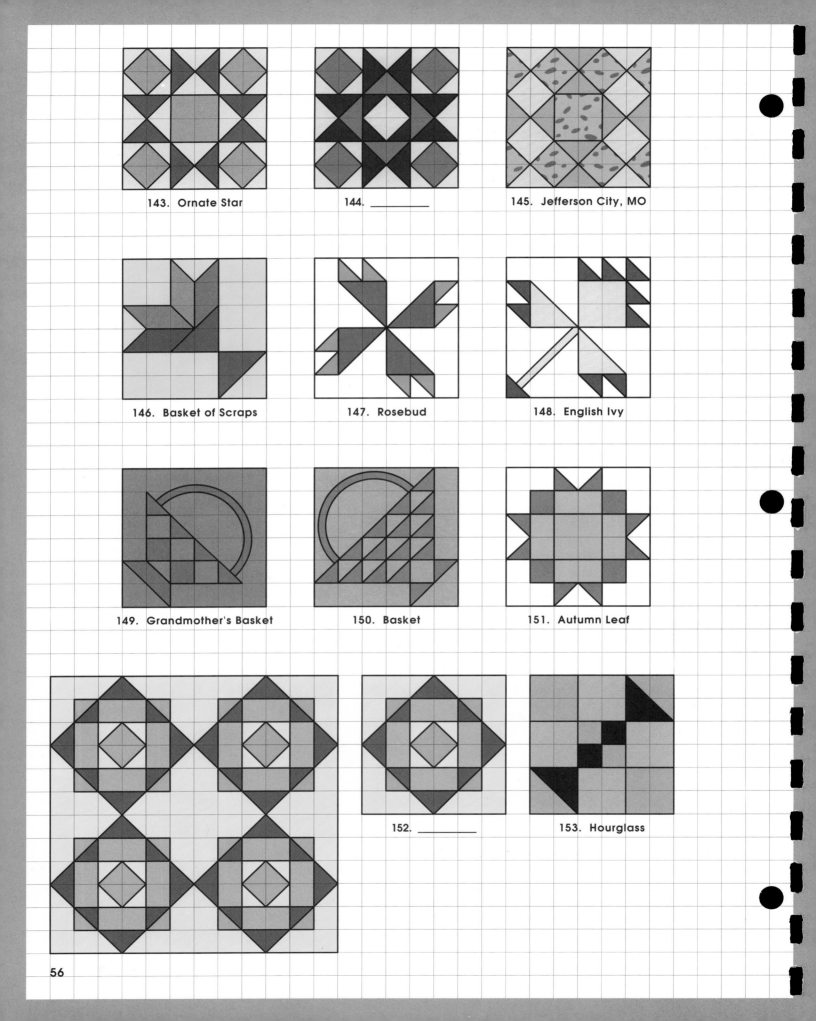

143. Ornate Star

144. _____

145. Jefferson City, MO

146. Basket of Scraps

147. Rosebud

148. English Ivy

149. Grandmother's Basket

150. Basket

151. Autumn Leaf

152. _____

153. Hourglass

56

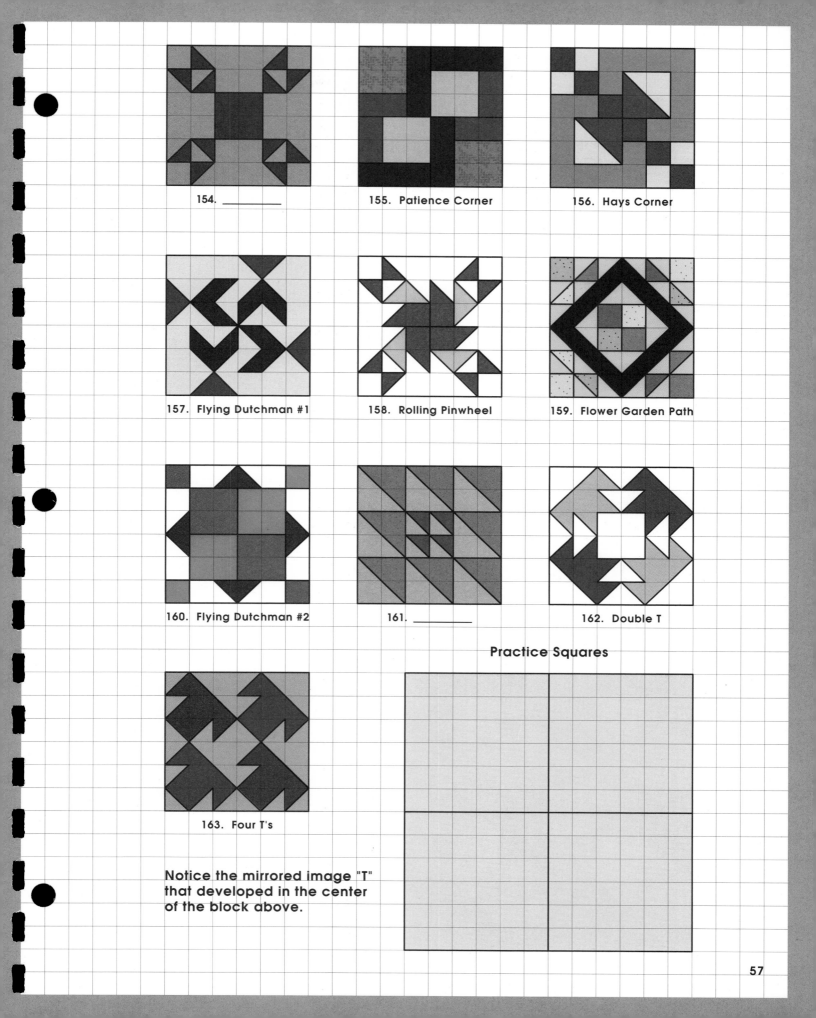

154. _____

155. Patience Corner

156. Hays Corner

157. Flying Dutchman #1

158. Rolling Pinwheel

159. Flower Garden Path

160. Flying Dutchman #2

161. _____

162. Double T

Practice Squares

163. Four T's

Notice the mirrored image "T" that developed in the center of the block above.

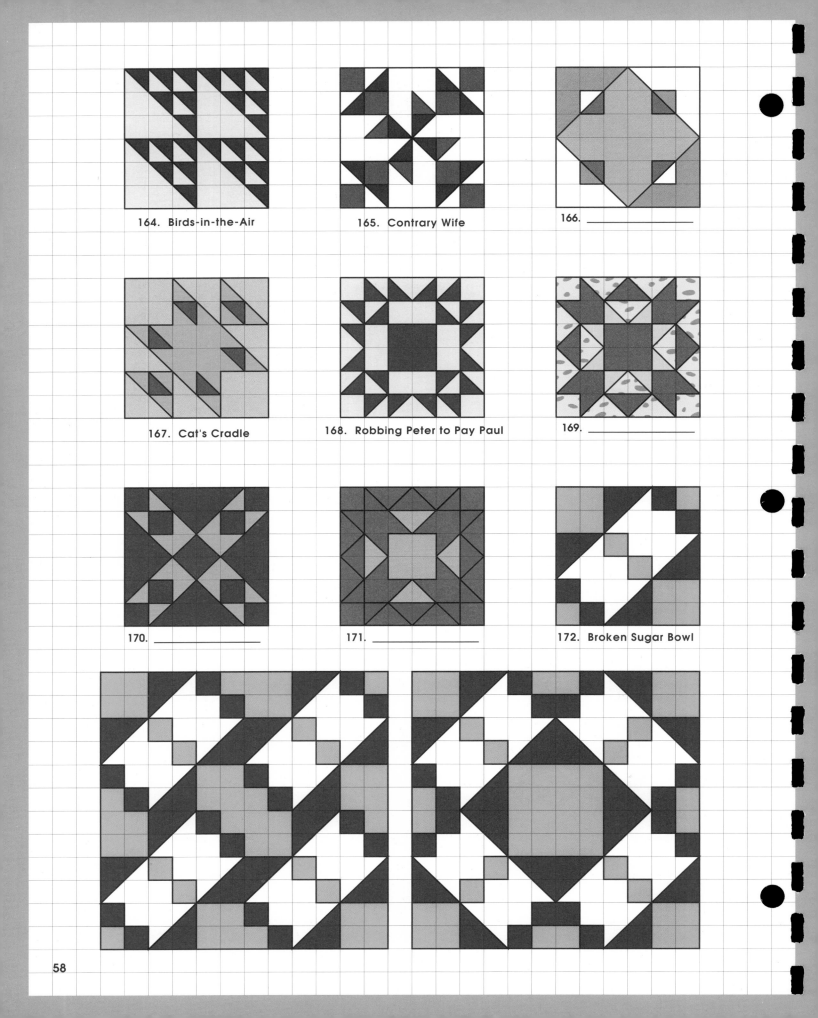

164. Birds-in-the-Air

165. Contrary Wife

166. _____

167. Cat's Cradle

168. Robbing Peter to Pay Paul

169. _____

170. _____

171. _____

172. Broken Sugar Bowl

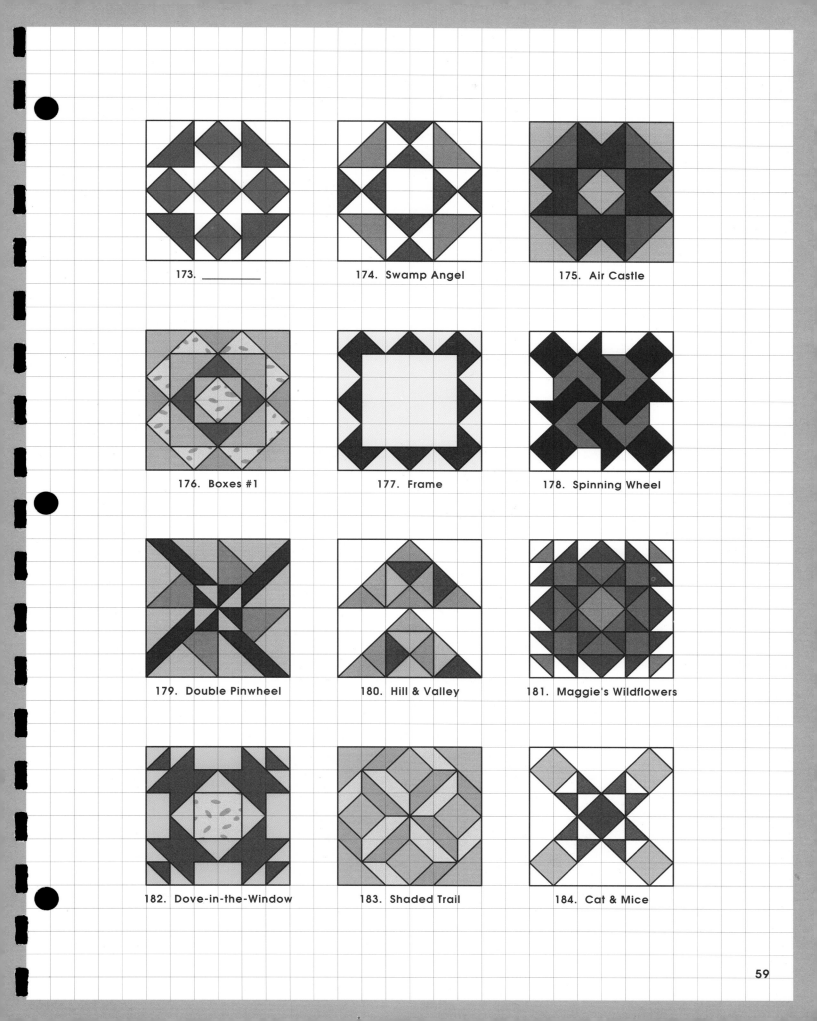

173. _____

174. Swamp Angel

175. Air Castle

176. Boxes #1

177. Frame

178. Spinning Wheel

179. Double Pinwheel

180. Hill & Valley

181. Maggie's Wildflowers

182. Dove-in-the-Window

183. Shaded Trail

184. Cat & Mice

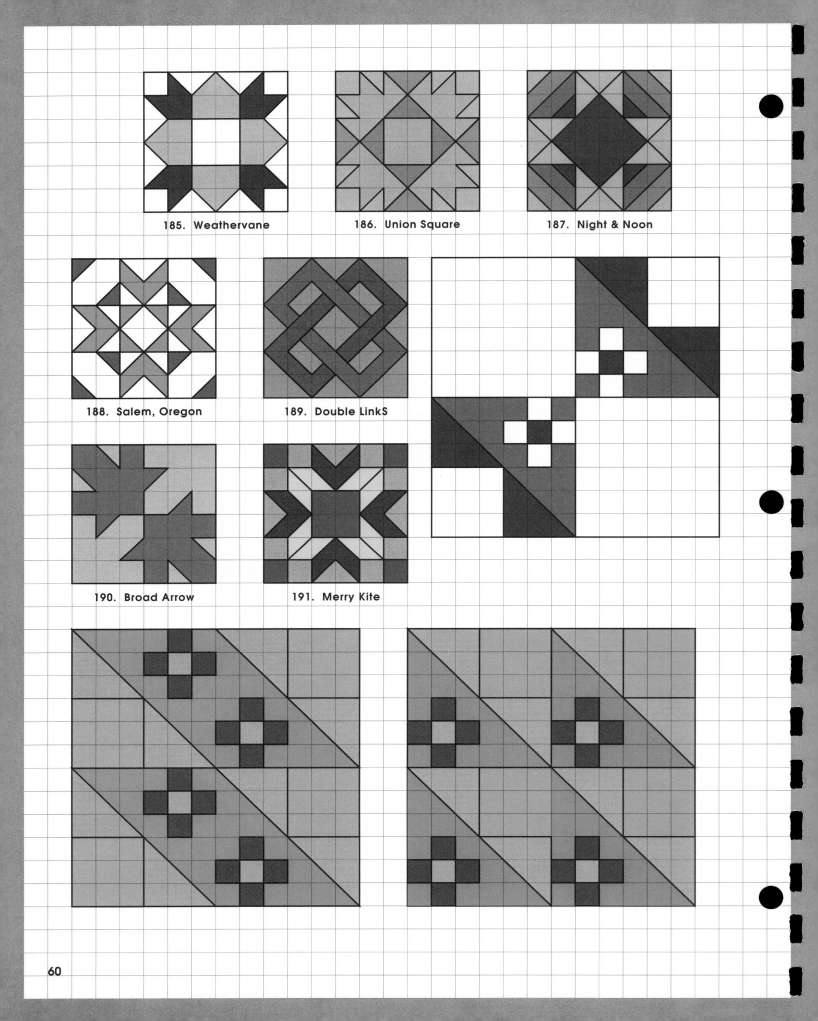

185. Weathervane

186. Union Square

187. Night & Noon

188. Salem, Oregon

189. Double LinkS

190. Broad Arrow

191. Merry Kite

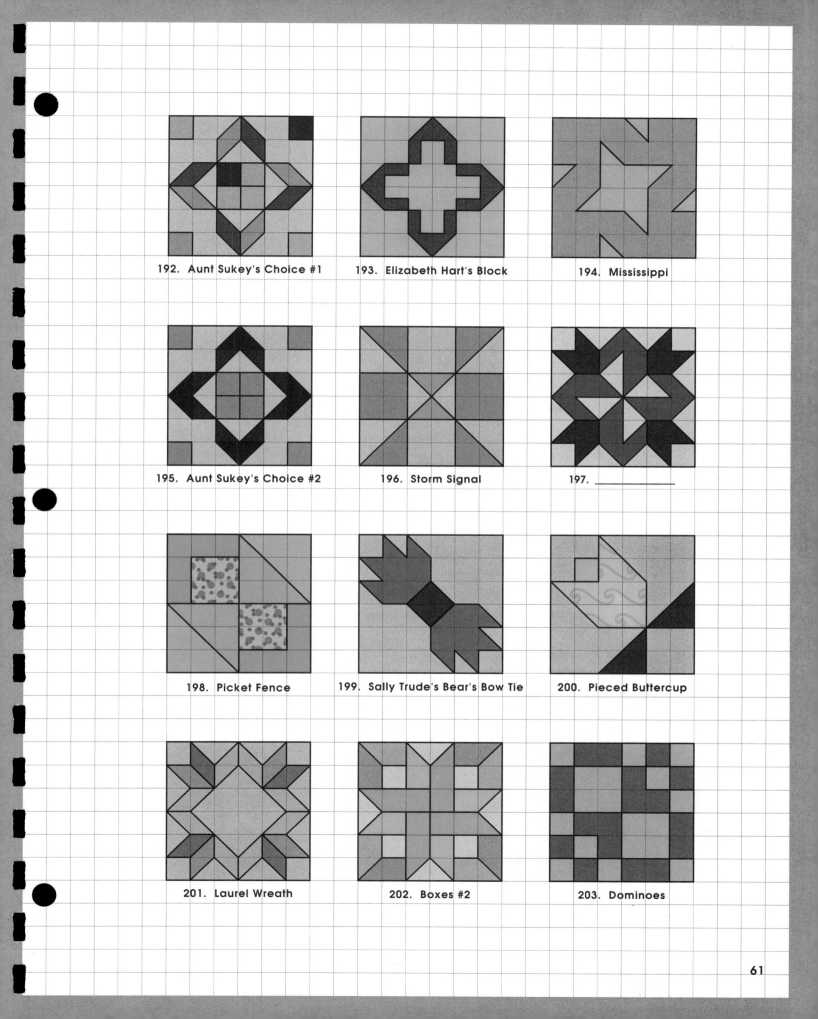

192. Aunt Sukey's Choice #1

193. Elizabeth Hart's Block

194. Mississippi

195. Aunt Sukey's Choice #2

196. Storm Signal

197. _____

198. Picket Fence

199. Sally Trude's Bear's Bow Tie

200. Pieced Buttercup

201. Laurel Wreath

202. Boxes #2

203. Dominoes

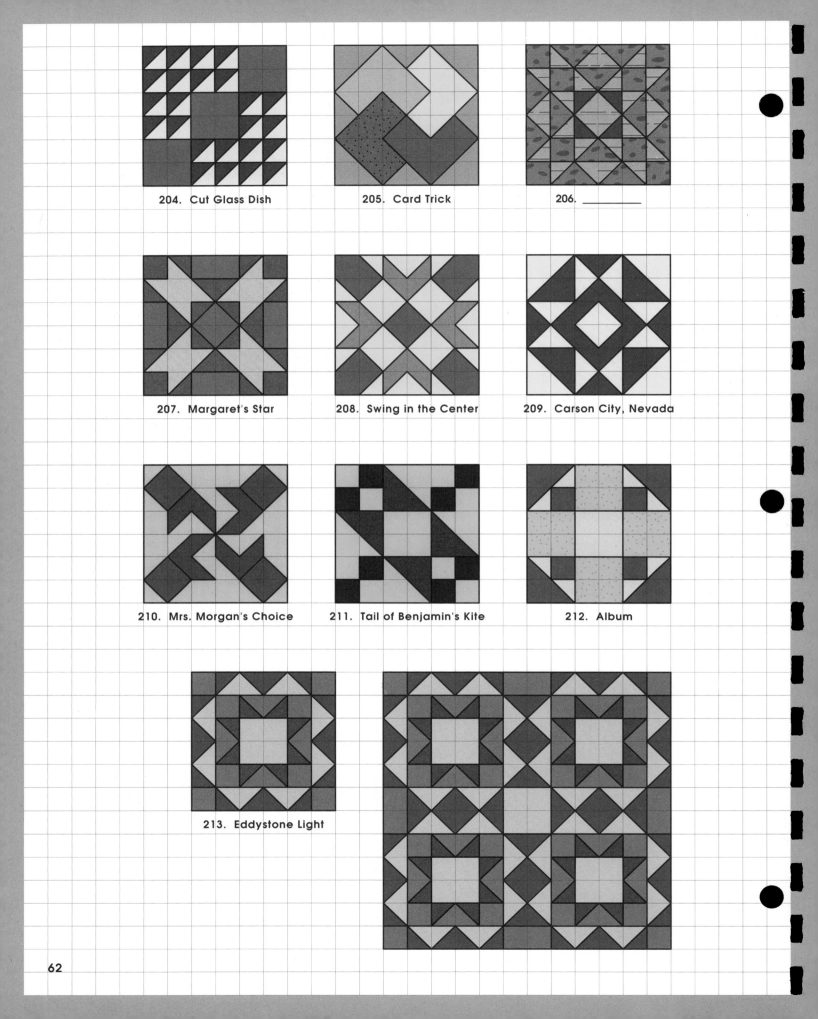

204. Cut Glass Dish

205. Card Trick

206. _____

207. Margaret's Star

208. Swing in the Center

209. Carson City, Nevada

210. Mrs. Morgan's Choice

211. Tail of Benjamin's Kite

212. Album

213. Eddystone Light

Seven Patch

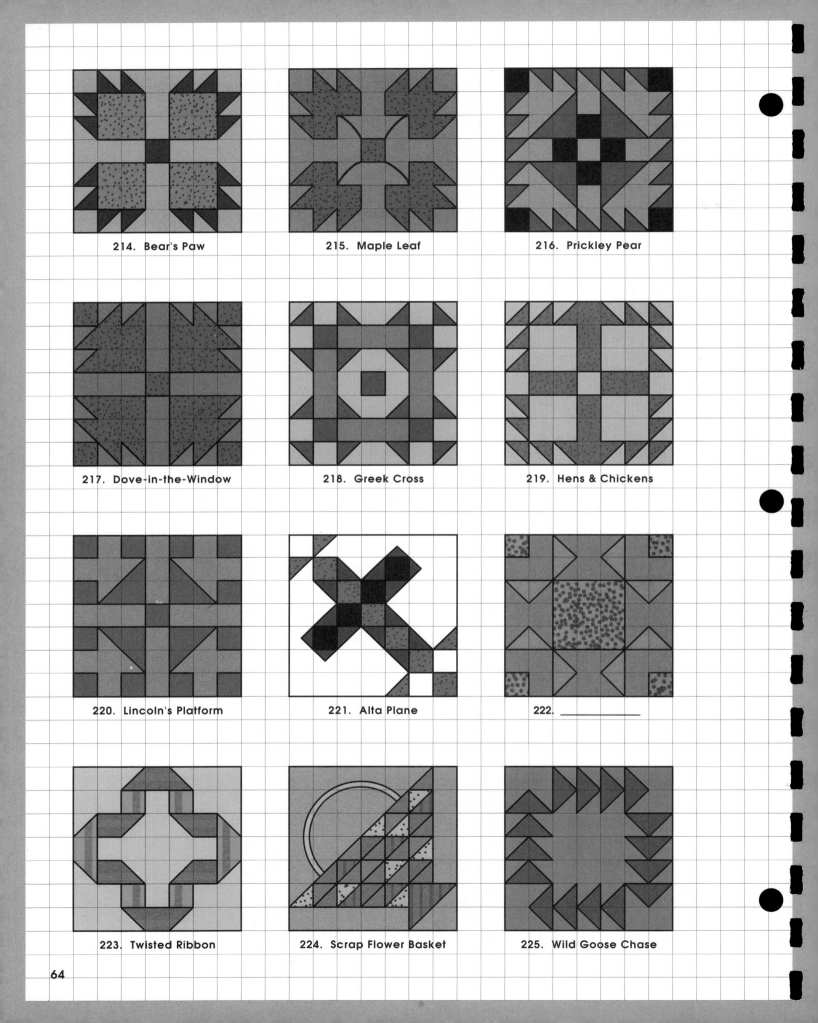

214. Bear's Paw

215. Maple Leaf

216. Prickley Pear

217. Dove-in-the-Window

218. Greek Cross

219. Hens & Chickens

220. Lincoln's Platform

221. Alta Plane

222. _____

223. Twisted Ribbon

224. Scrap Flower Basket

225. Wild Goose Chase

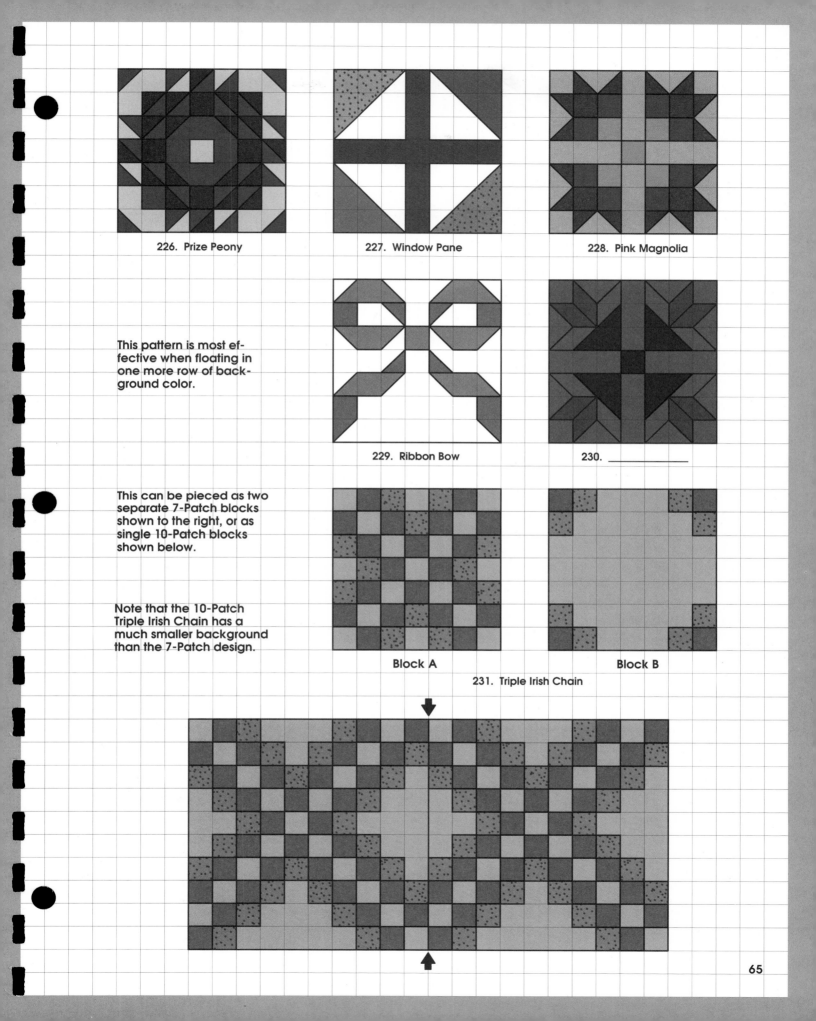

226. Prize Peony

227. Window Pane

228. Pink Magnolia

This pattern is most effective when floating in one more row of background color.

229. Ribbon Bow

230. _____

This can be pieced as two separate 7-Patch blocks shown to the right, or as single 10-Patch blocks shown below.

Note that the 10-Patch Triple Irish Chain has a much smaller background than the 7-Patch design.

Block A

Block B

231. Triple Irish Chain

65

66

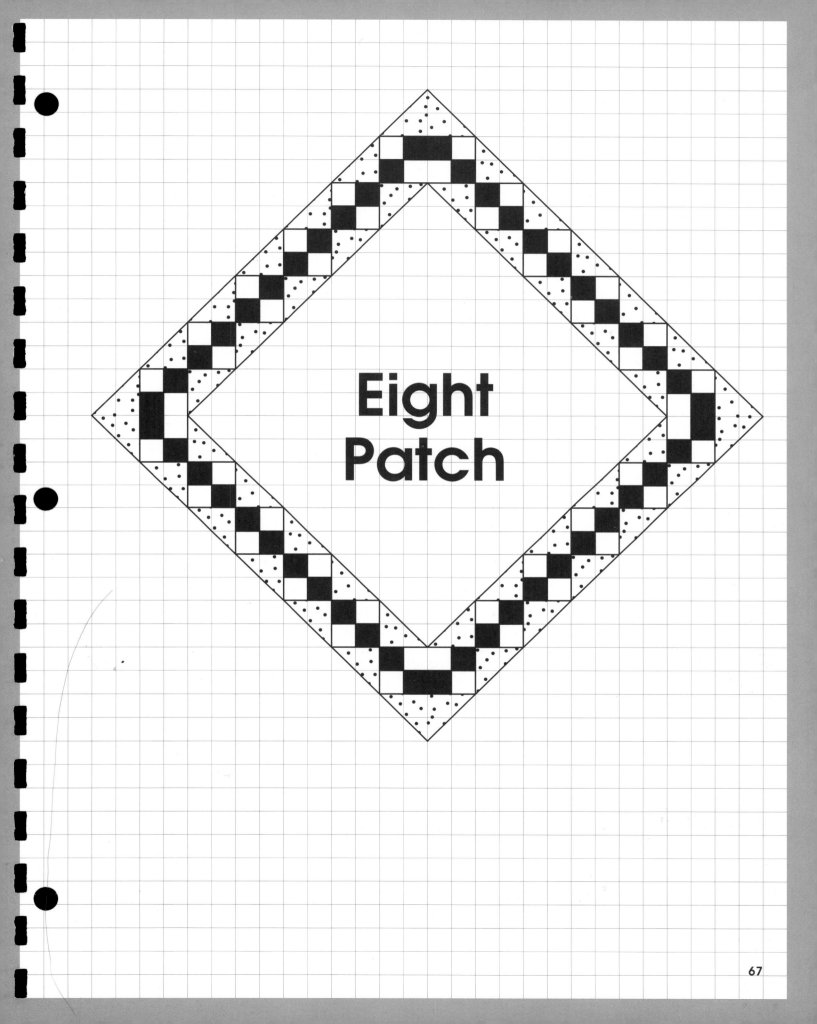

Eight
Patch

232. Jewels in a Frame

233. _____

234. Indian Trails & Irish Puzzle

235. Kansas Troubles

236. Barrister's Block

237. Delectable Mountains

238. Devil's Claw

239. Year's Favorite

240. Eternal Triangle

241. Fancy Windmill

242. Indian Hatchet

243. Crow's Foot

244. Enclosed Stars

245. Path Through the Woods

246. Chinese Puzzle

247. Stepping Stones

248. Odd Fellows Chain

249. Blackford's Beauty

250. Robbing Peter to Pay Paul

251. Northumberland Star

252. Martha Washington's Star

253. Square & Stars

254. Diamond Star

255. Eight Hands Around

256. Navajo

257. Albany, New York

258. West Virginia

259. Baton Rouge, Louisiana

260. Marion's Choice

261. Gretchen

262. Jack-in-the-Pulpit

263. Memory Chain

264. Casey's Camp

265. Georgetown Circle
or Crown of Thorns

266. Fanny's Favorite

267. Grandmother's Favorite

70

268. World's Fair

269. Flying Clouds

270. Sunny Lanes

271. Starry Path #1

272. Starry Path #2

273. World's Fair Block

274. Wheel of Fortune

275. Show Off

276. The Rambler

277. Carpenter's Wheel Variation

278. The Broken Path
Kansas City Star, Oct. 25, 1939

279. Irene Gutzeit's Iris Rainbow

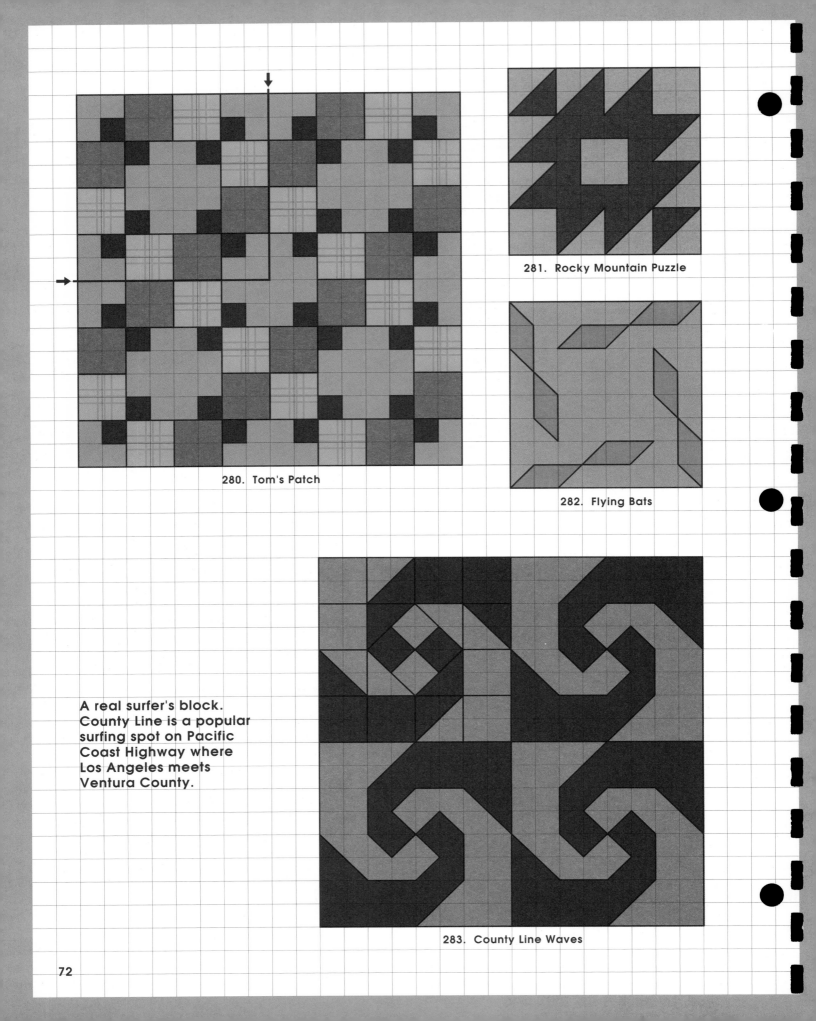

280. Tom's Patch

281. Rocky Mountain Puzzle

282. Flying Bats

A real surfer's block. County Line is a popular surfing spot on Pacific Coast Highway where Los Angeles meets Ventura County.

283. County Line Waves

Nine
Patch

284. Tile

285. Alabama

286. Puss-in-the-Corner

287. Butterfly

288. Alice's Favorite

289. Jackson, Mississippi
or Prosperity Block

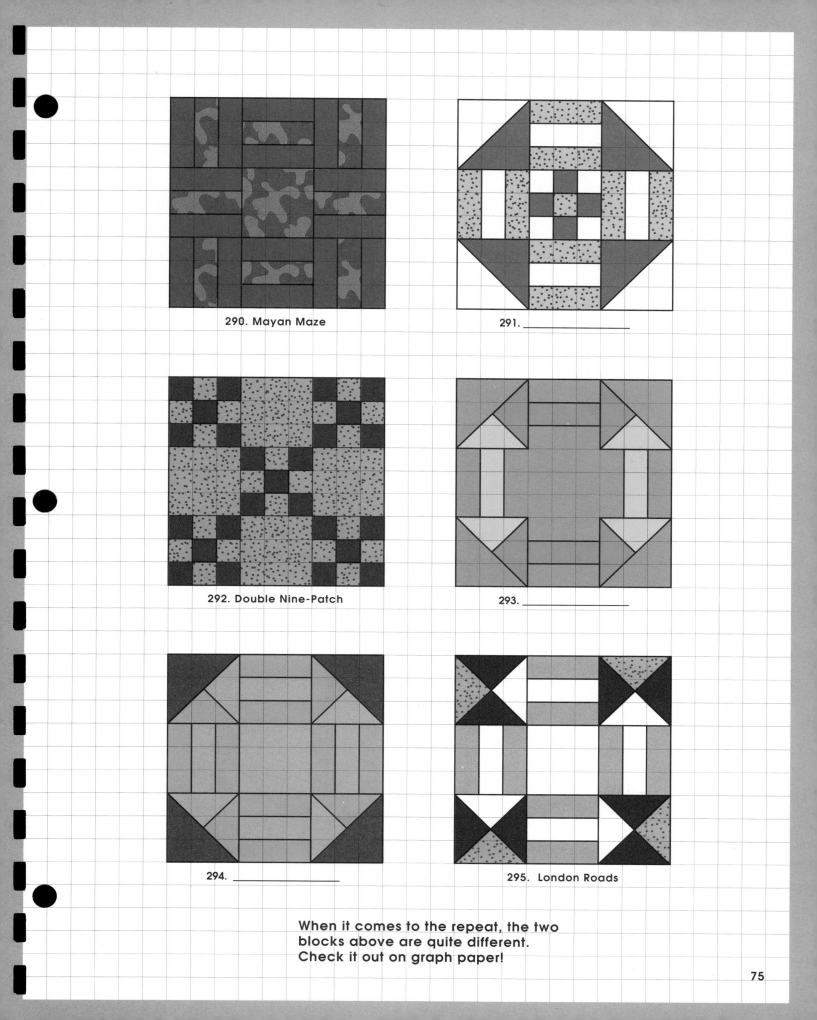

290. Mayan Maze

291. _____

292. Double Nine-Patch

293. _____

294. _____

295. London Roads

When it comes to the repeat, the two
blocks above are quite different.
Check it out on graph paper!

75

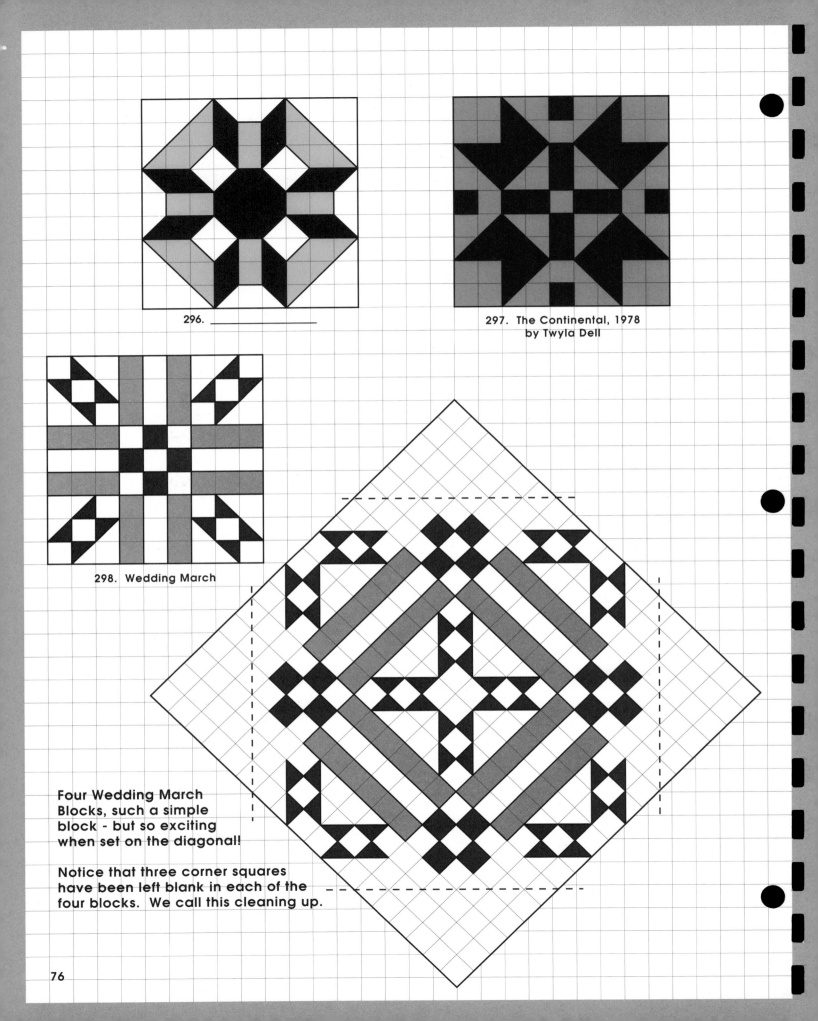

296. _____

297. The Continental, 1978
by Twyla Dell

298. Wedding March

Four Wedding March
Blocks, such a simple
block - but so exciting
when set on the diagonal!

Notice that three corner squares
have been left blank in each of the
four blocks. We call this cleaning up.

Ten
Patch

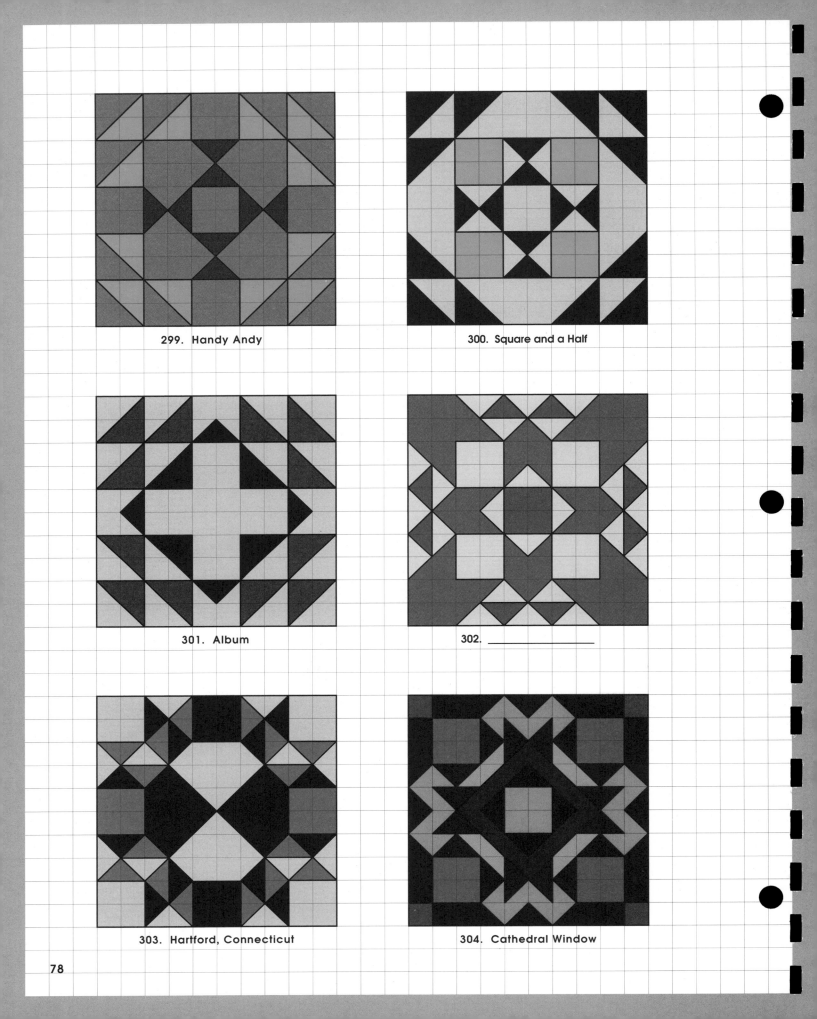

299. Handy Andy

300. Square and a Half

301. Album

302. _____

303. Hartford, Connecticut

304. Cathedral Window

305. Katie's Favorite

306. Bird's Nest

307. Mother's Fancy Star

308. Milky Way

This is really an 8-Patch pattern when used to develop a repeat (see arrows).

It is a 10-Patch when making the self-contained positive-negative pattern shown here.

309. Wood Lily or Indian Head

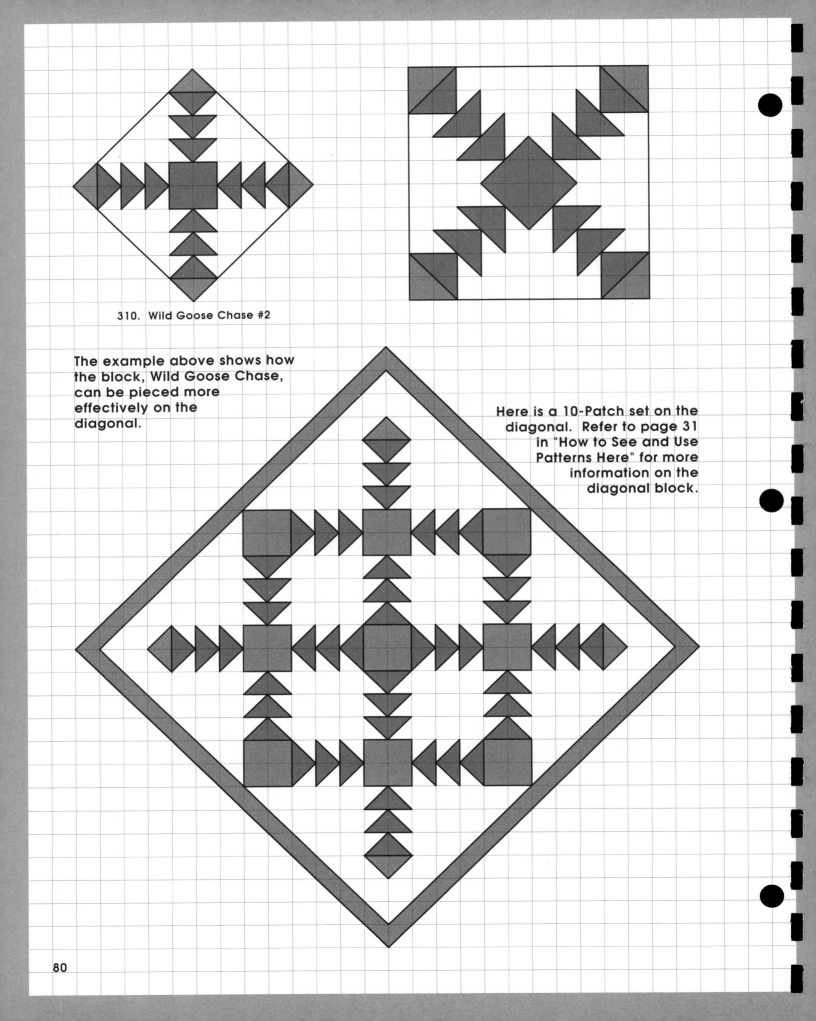

310. Wild Goose Chase #2

The example above shows how
the block, Wild Goose Chase,
can be pieced more
effectively on the
diagonal.

Here is a 10-Patch set on the
diagonal. Refer to page 31
in "How to See and Use
Patterns Here" for more
information on the
diagonal block.

Eleven and Twelve Patch

311. Interlaced Blocks

312. Dove at my Window

313. South Dakota

314. Christmas Star

315. Grandmother's Dream

316. Blazing Star

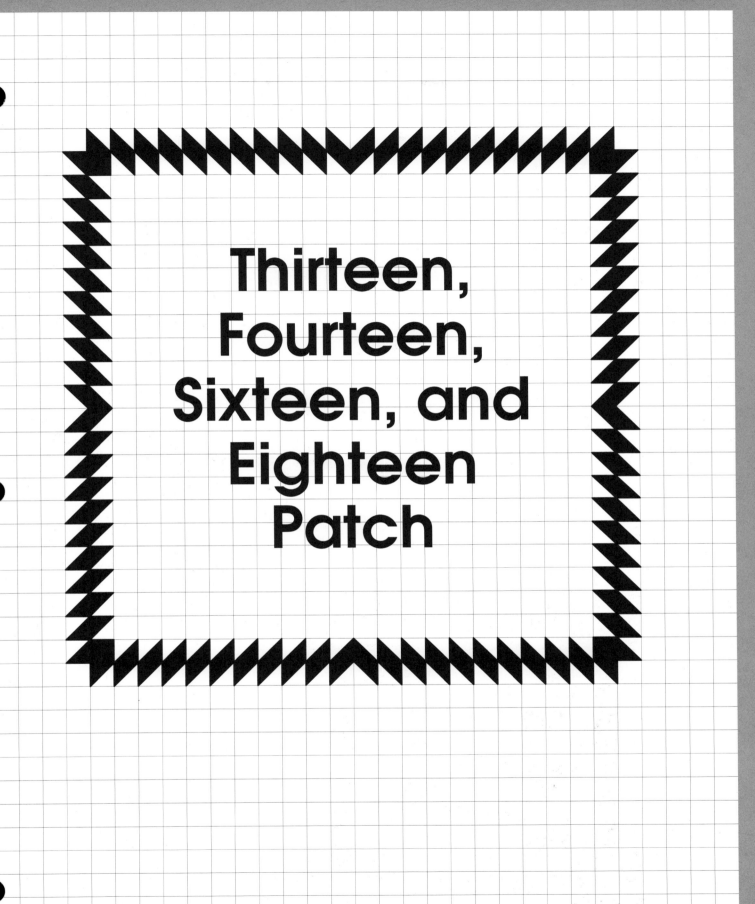

Thirteen, Fourteen, Sixteen, and Eighteen Patch

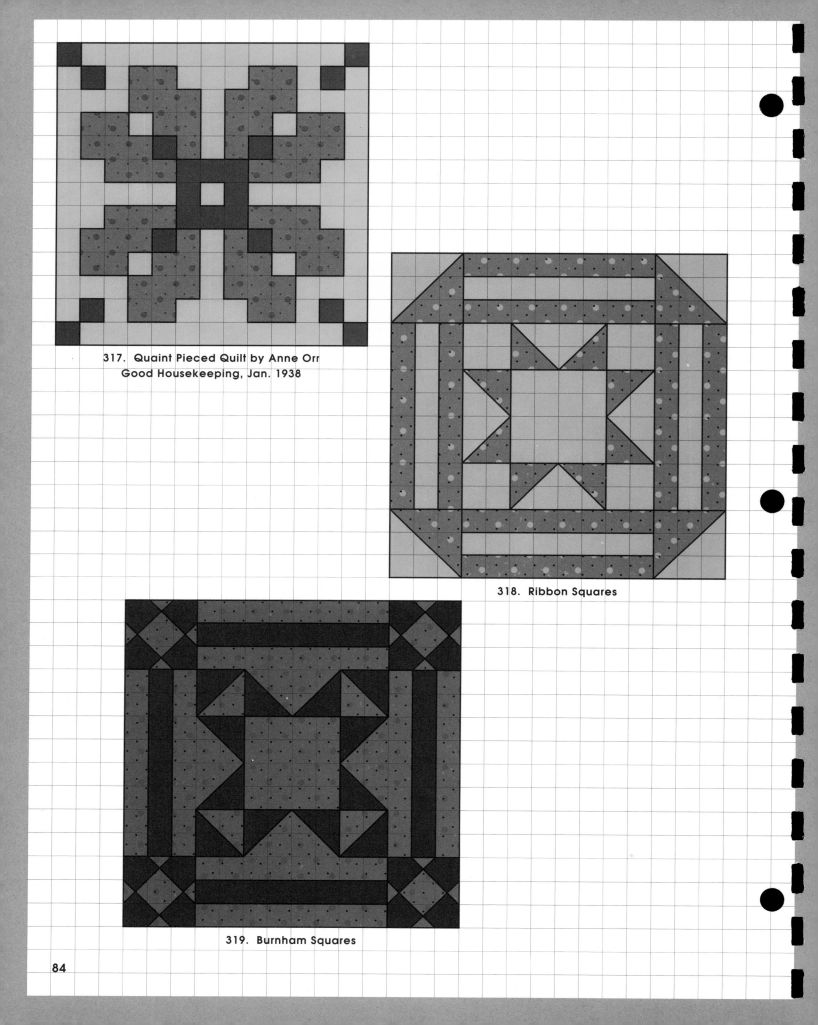

317. Quaint Pieced Quilt by Anne Orr
Good Housekeeping, Jan. 1938

318. Ribbon Squares

319. Burnham Squares

320. Four Queens

321. Feathered Star
(simplified version)

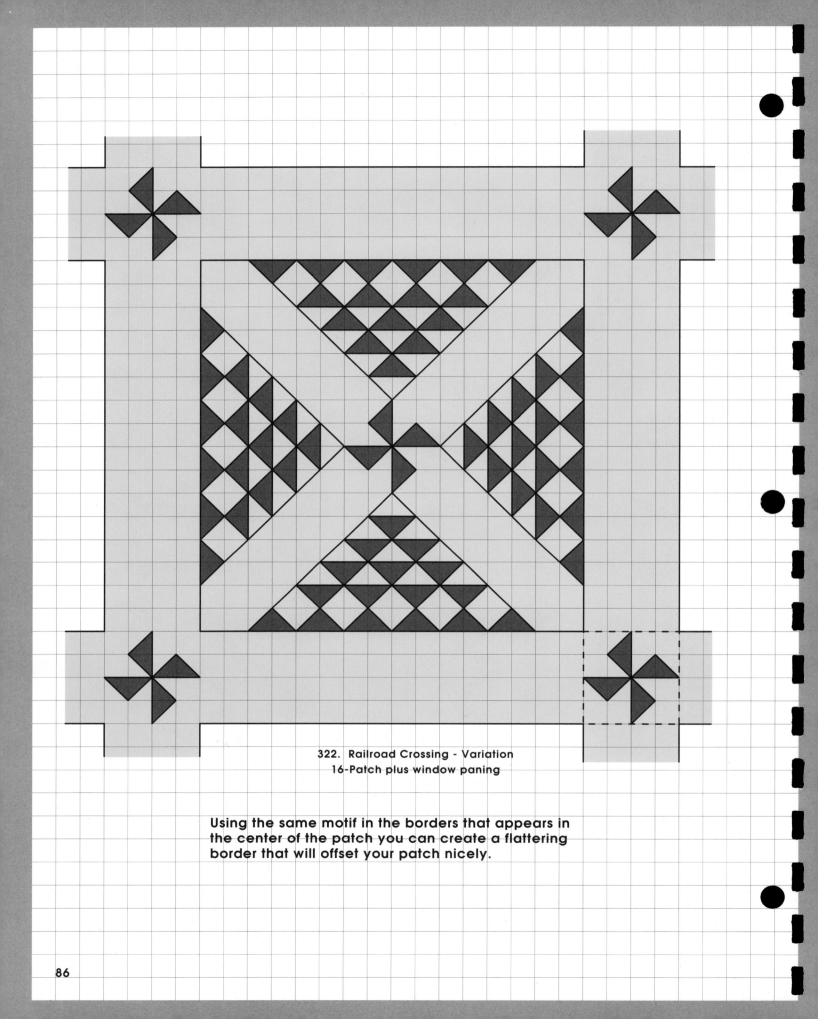

322. Railroad Crossing - Variation
16-Patch plus window paning

Using the same motif in the borders that appears in
the center of the patch you can create a flattering
border that will offset your patch nicely.

Trees, Roads, Crosses and More!

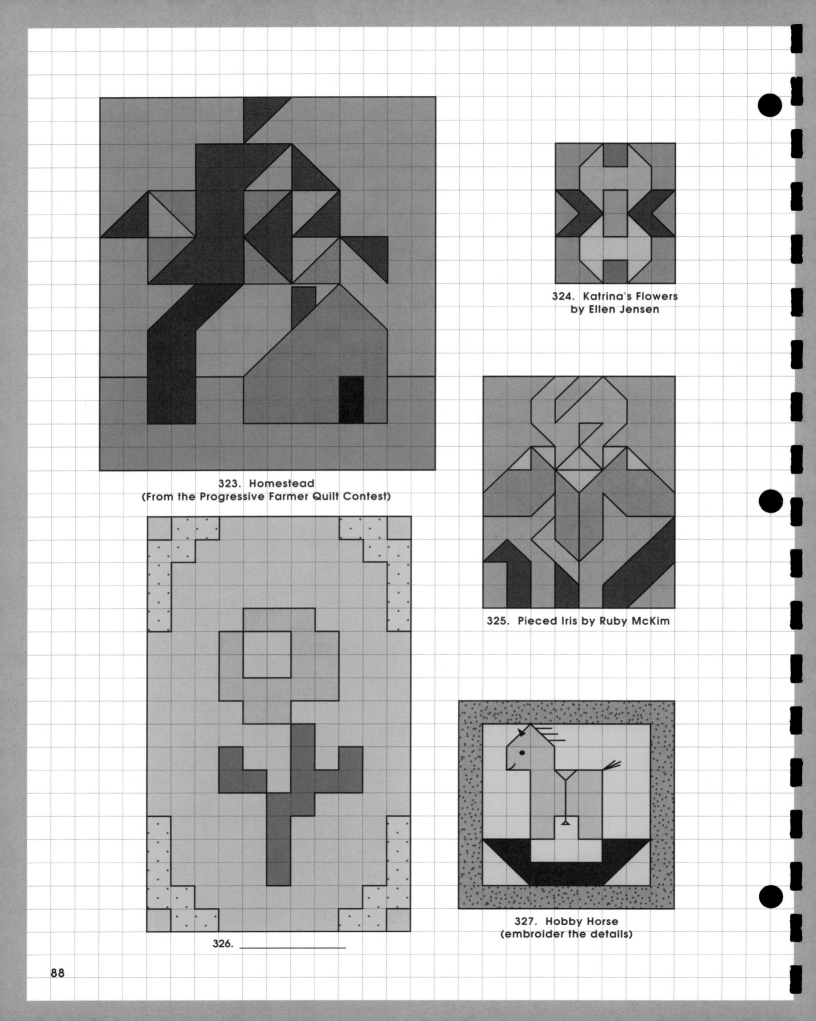

323. Homestead
(From the Progressive Farmer Quilt Contest)

324. Katrina's Flowers
by Ellen Jensen

325. Pieced Iris by Ruby McKim

326. _____

327. Hobby Horse
(embroider the details)

Trees

Here is an example of how one motif can be used to create many variations.

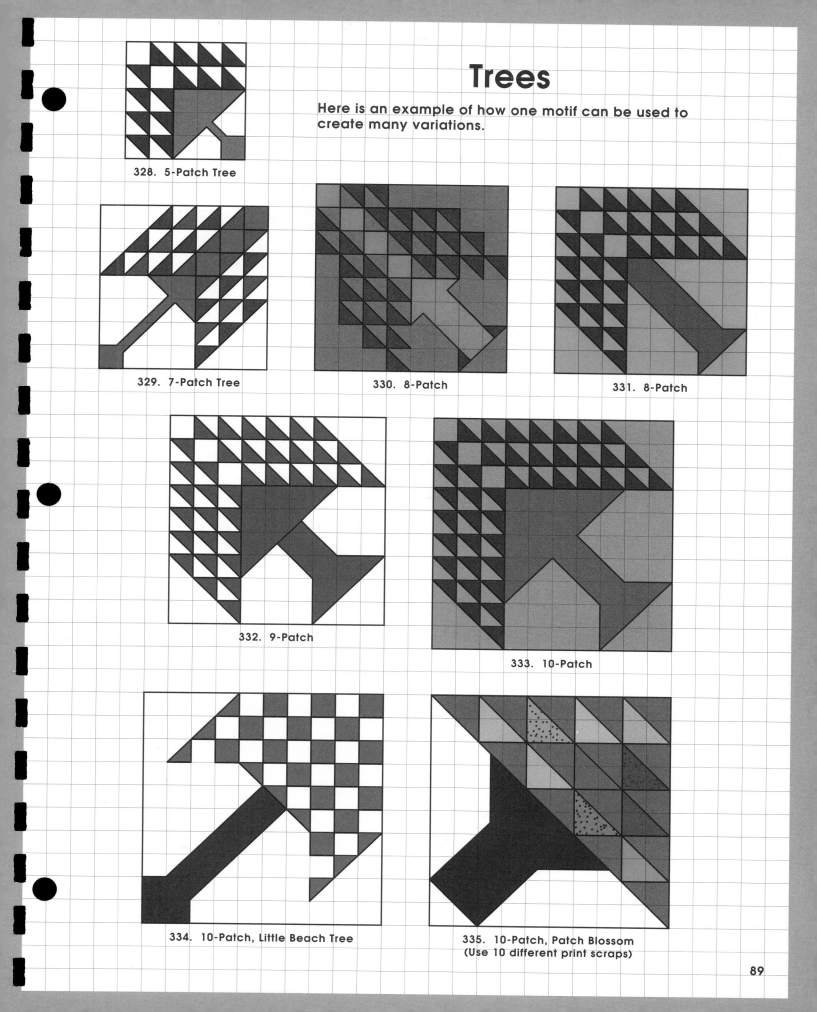

328. 5-Patch Tree

329. 7-Patch Tree

330. 8-Patch

331. 8-Patch

332. 9-Patch

333. 10-Patch

334. 10-Patch, Little Beach Tree

335. 10-Patch, Patch Blossom
(Use 10 different print scraps)

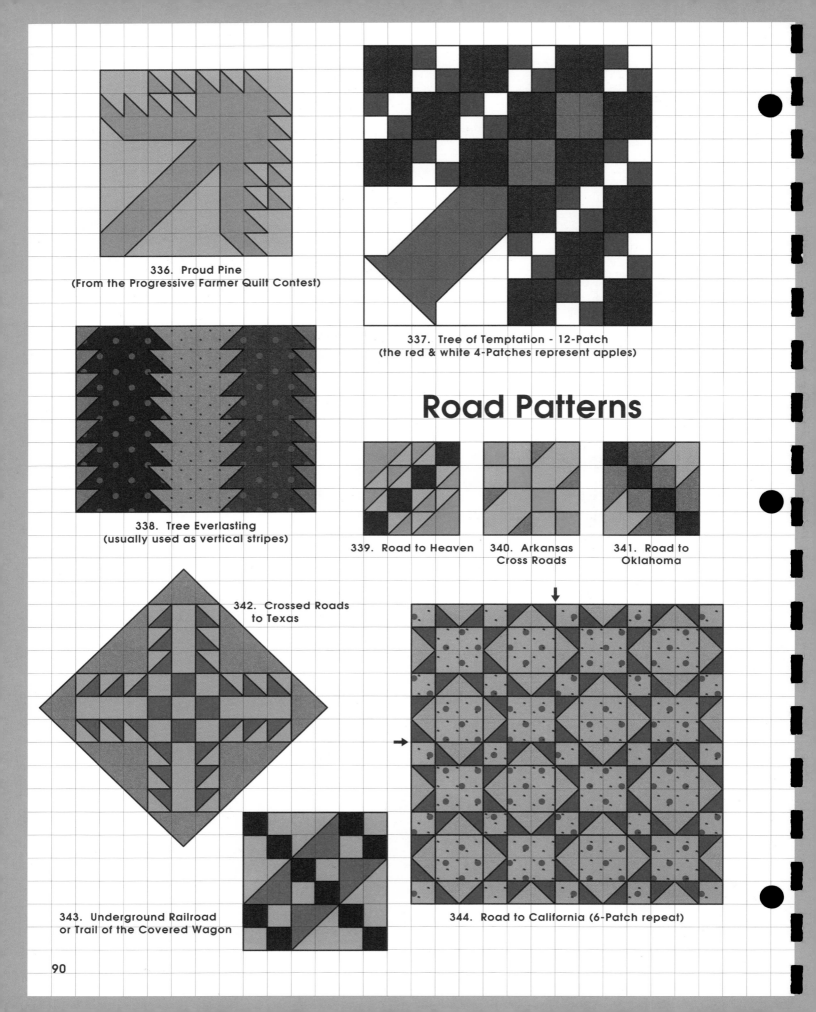

336. Proud Pine
(From the Progressive Farmer Quilt Contest)

337. Tree of Temptation - 12-Patch
(the red & white 4-Patches represent apples)

338. Tree Everlasting
(usually used as vertical stripes)

Road Patterns

339. Road to Heaven

340. Arkansas
Cross Roads

341. Road to
Oklahoma

342. Crossed Roads
to Texas

343. Underground Railroad
or Trail of the Covered Wagon

344. Road to California (6-Patch repeat)

The patterns on this page are popular for "album" type quilts with signatures in the center.

345. _____

346. Memory Block

347. Domino & Square
(1st Shading)

348. Arbor Window

349. Domino & Square
(2nd Shading)

"Album" Patterns

350. Roman Cross

351. Christian Cross

352. Washington Sidewalks

354. Rocky Glen

355. _____

353. _____

356. This is a fantastic frame!

357. Sparkling Star

Looking at a Pattern Two Different Ways

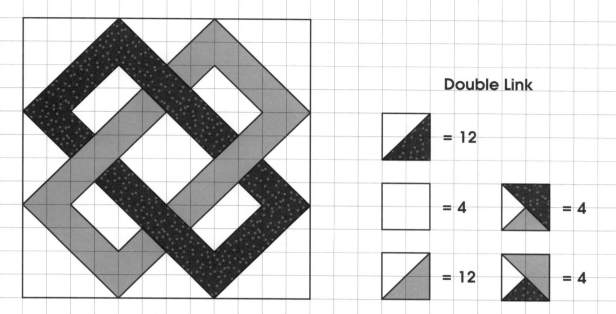

Double Link

Here is a Double Links as a Six-Patch made up of triangles. It would be a knockout made as a scrap quilt - for instance, one link made up of different navy blues, the other made up of all different greens. The background should stay constant.

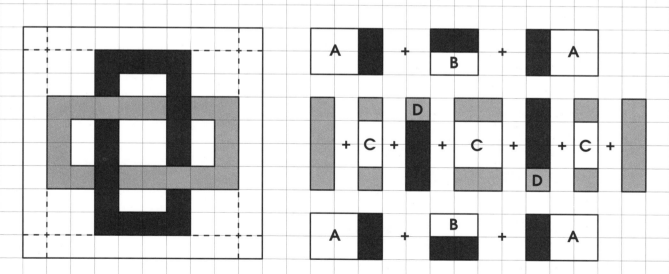

Here is a quick and easy way to piece the Double Links. Sewing the strips together will create the Double Links as above, but each link should be all one color. By setting these blocks on the diagonal, you achieve the same look as the first block.

Borders

Here are some samples of borders that are easy to piece together.

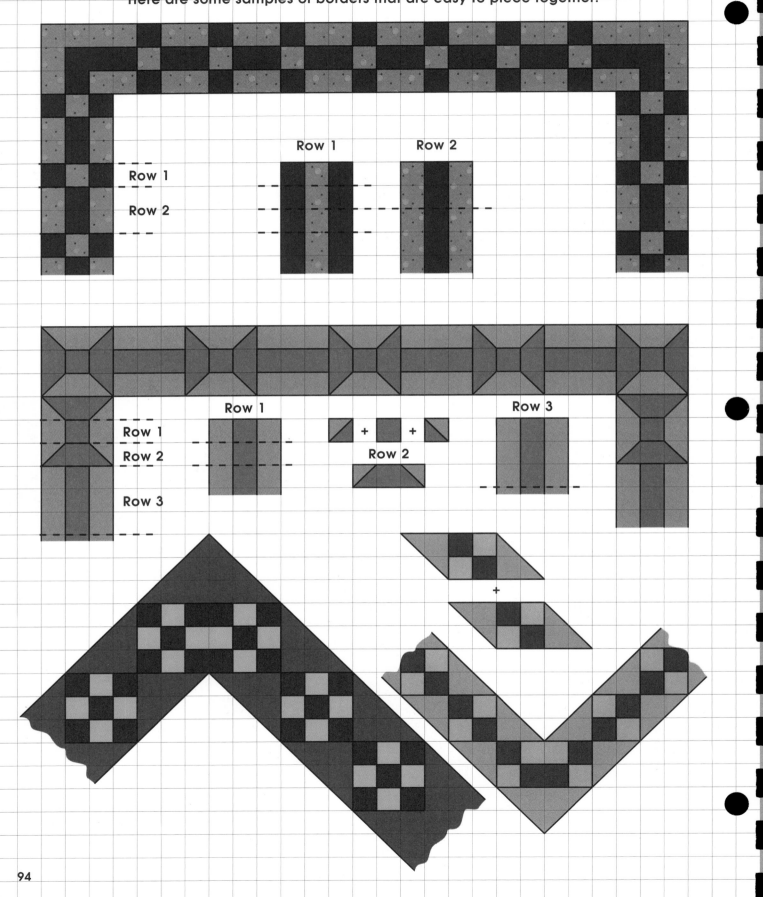

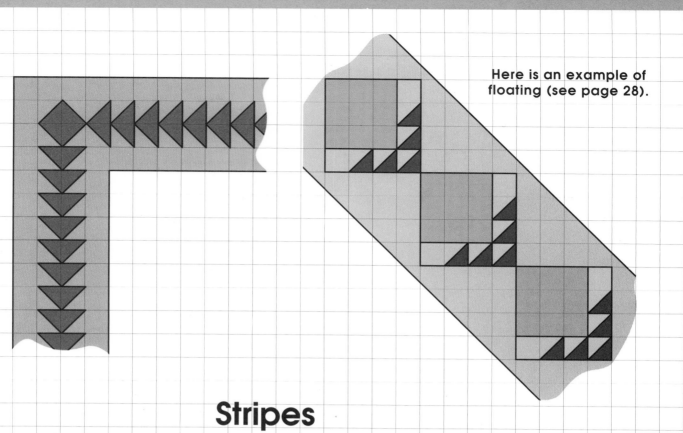

Here is an example of floating (see page 28).

Stripes

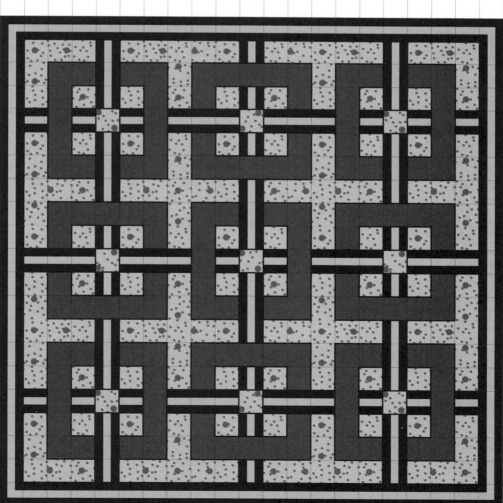

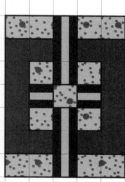

The Block

Notice how the positioning of the blocks creates a woven pattern.

Fancy 3-Patch Chain

To see the pattern in this quilt you should stand at least 10 feet away after it has been pieced together.

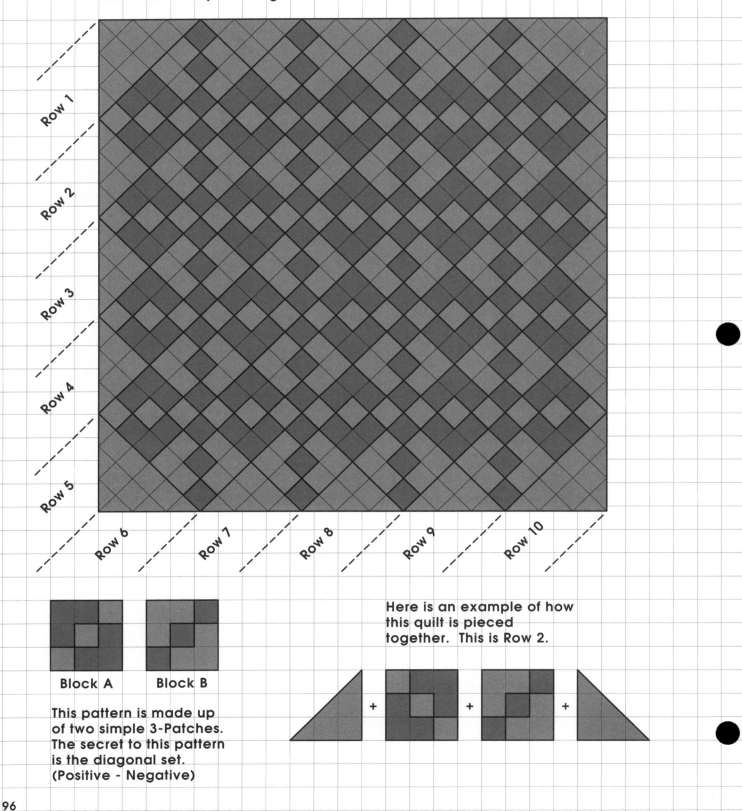

Block A **Block B**

This pattern is made up of two simple 3-Patches. The secret to this pattern is the diagonal set. (Positive - Negative)

Here is an example of how this quilt is pieced together. This is Row 2.

Fancy 3-Patch Chain
(Bonus)

Hard to believe that such a simple little block - with different shadings and in a different set - can do such exciting things.

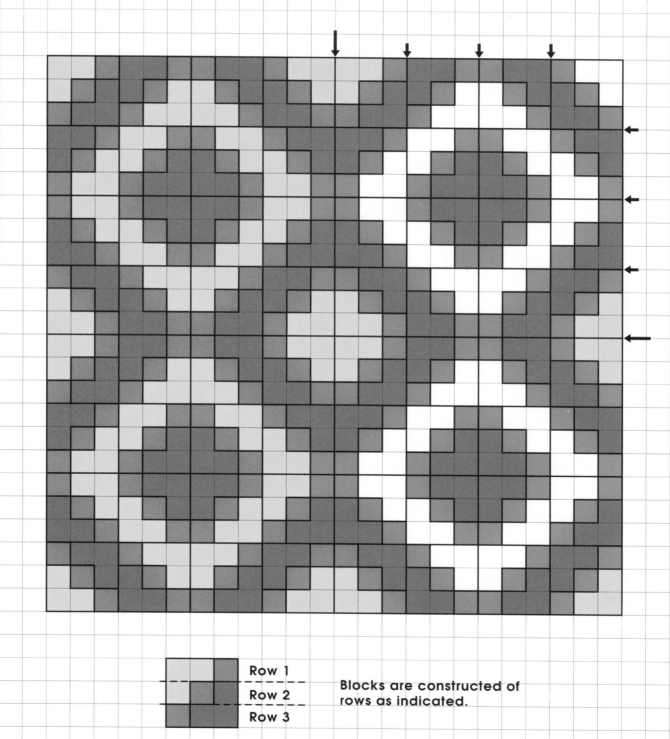

Row 1

Row 2

Row 3

Blocks are constructed of rows as indicated.

Shaded Triangles

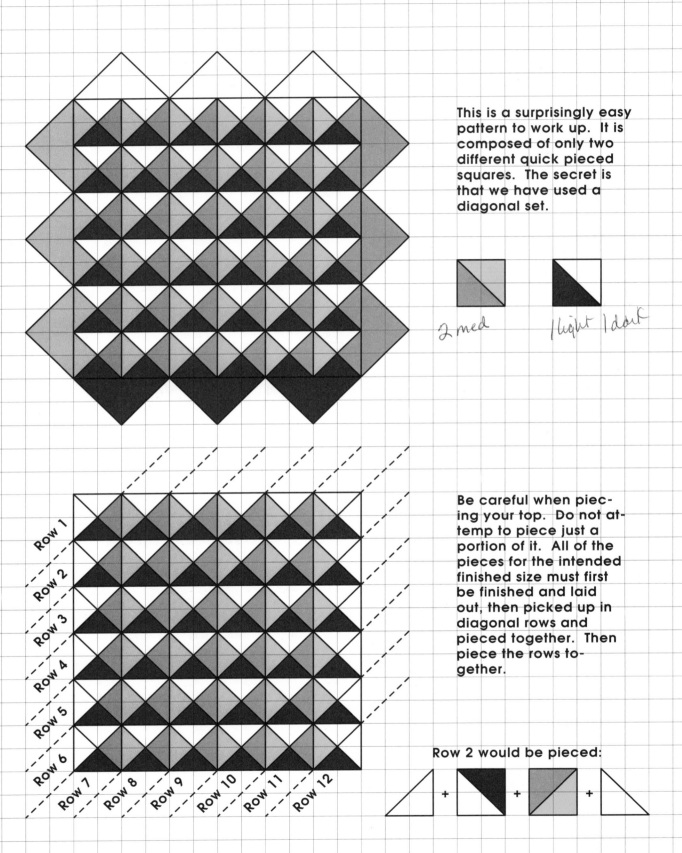

This is a surprisingly easy pattern to work up. It is composed of only two different quick pieced squares. The secret is that we have used a diagonal set.

2 med   1 light 1 dark

Be careful when piecing your top. Do not attemp to piece just a portion of it. All of the pieces for the intended finished size must first be finished and laid out, then picked up in diagonal rows and pieced together. Then piece the rows together.

Row 1
Row 2
Row 3
Row 4
Row 5
Row 6
Row 7 Row 8 Row 9 Row 10 Row 11 Row 12

Row 2 would be pieced:

+ + +

Shaded Triangles, continued

Row 1
Row 2
Row 3

High Sierra - An original pattern by Mary Ellen Hopkins

Four-Patch Christmas Holly Chain

Consider a diagonal set. This is the same block shaded two different ways.

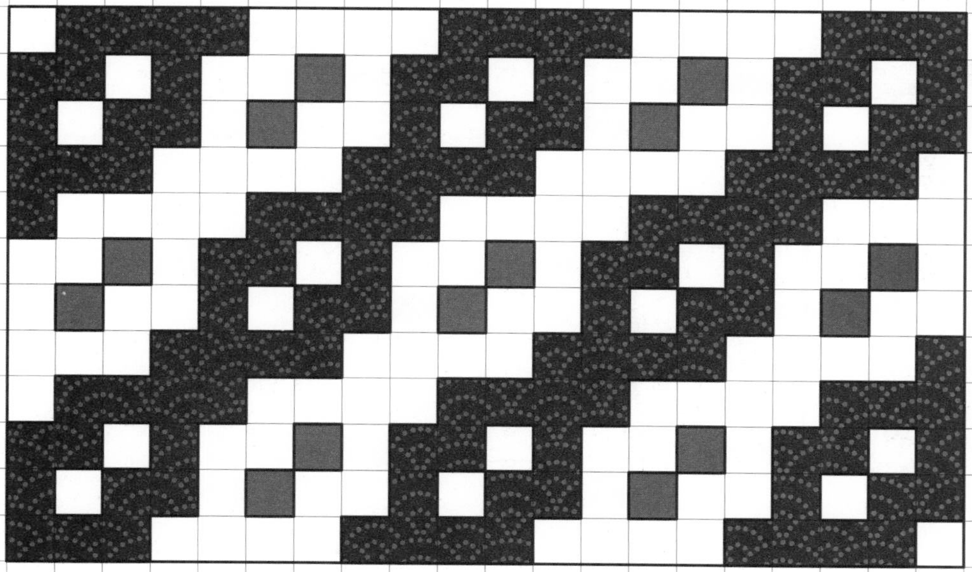

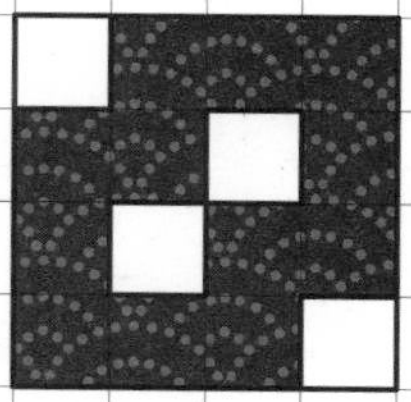

Block A

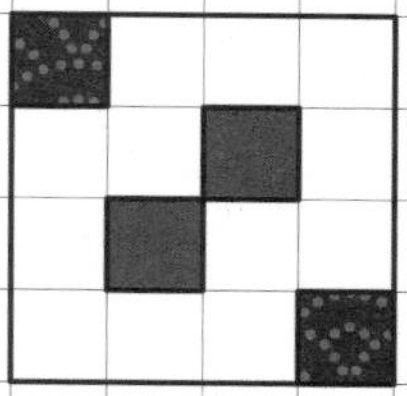

Block B

Variations

This is another gimmick. Take a simple pattern. Draw the repeat with no shading. Squint and you'll see different shapes emerging. Quick - color these shapes while you still see them. Look again and you'll probably see a different shape.

Try a combination of four repeats of a block, shaded as one. We'll talk about this again in the 9-Patch set-up.

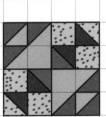

Old Maid's
Puzzle

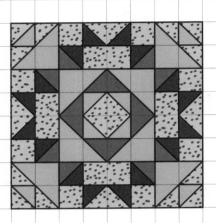

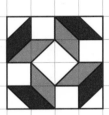

Bachelor's
Puzzle

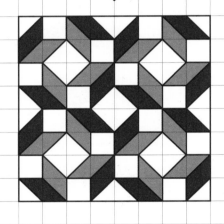

Shooting Stars

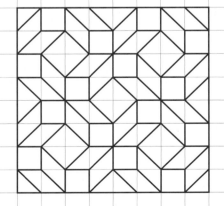

Now, you
squint and
fill it in.

Eight-Patch

The Laurel Wreath can be shaded many ways. These two examples are the same idea but different proportions.

Six-Patch

Positive-Negative

Gentleman's Fancy

For Your Eyes Only

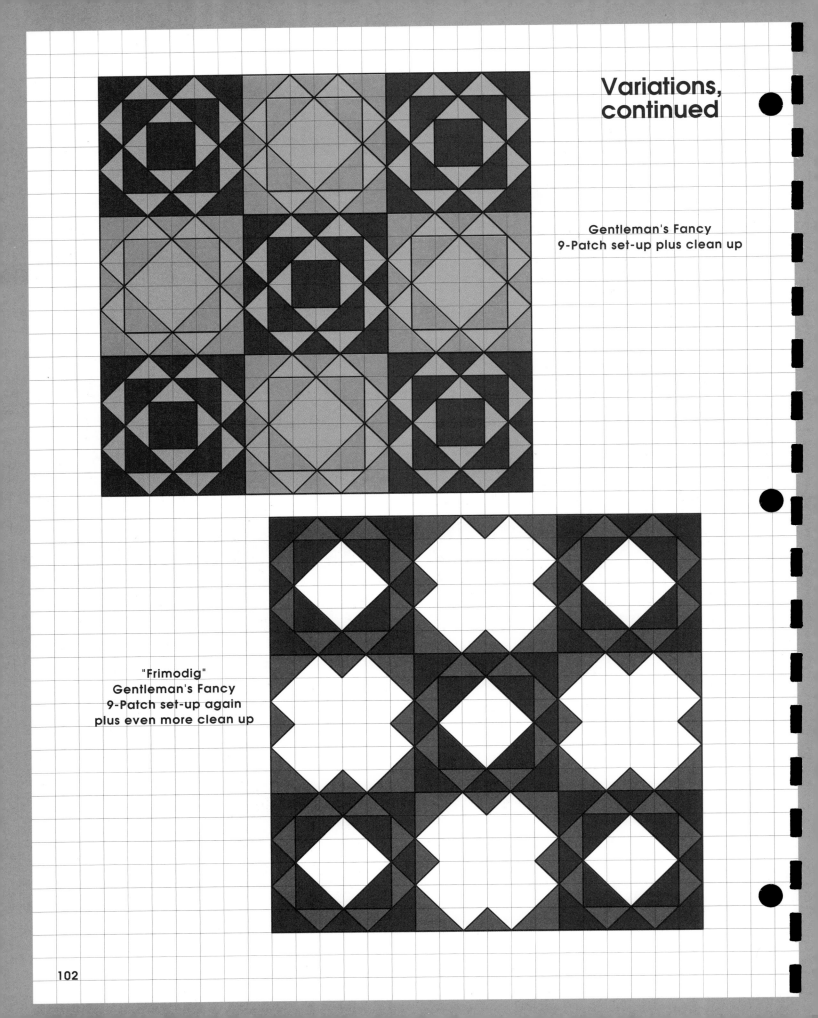

Gentleman's Fancy
9-Patch set-up plus clean up

"Frimodig"
Gentleman's Fancy
9-Patch set-up again
plus even more clean up

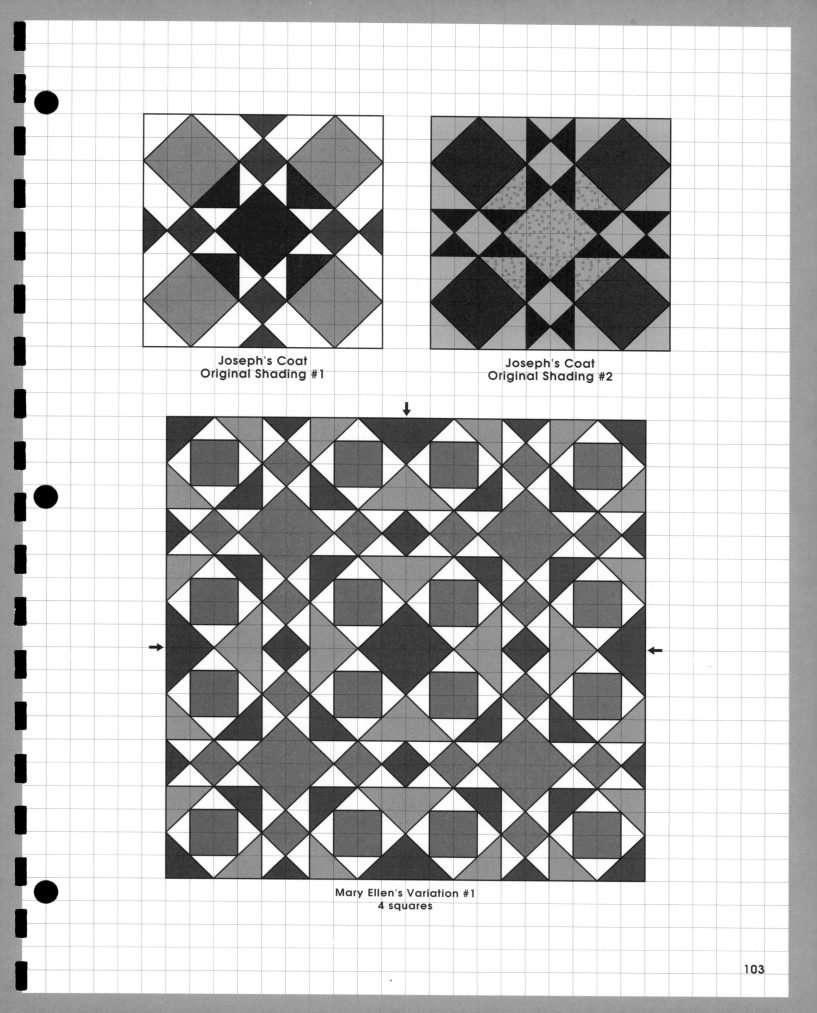

Joseph's Coat
Original Shading #1

Joseph's Coat
Original Shading #2

Mary Ellen's Variation #1
4 squares

Variations, continued

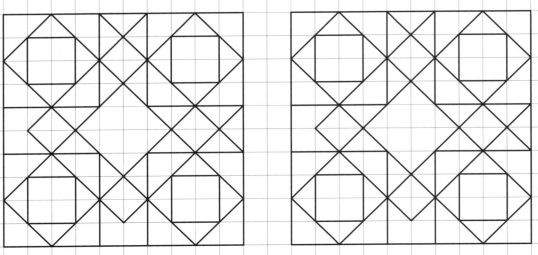

Try your own shadings for Joseph's Coat and see how different combinations of lights and darks can alter the design.

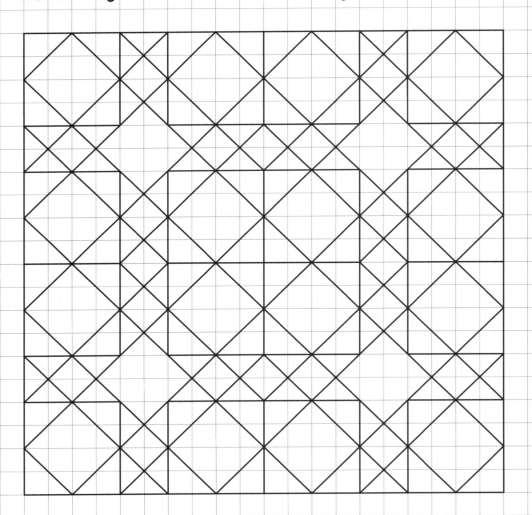

Remember, you can always take lines out!

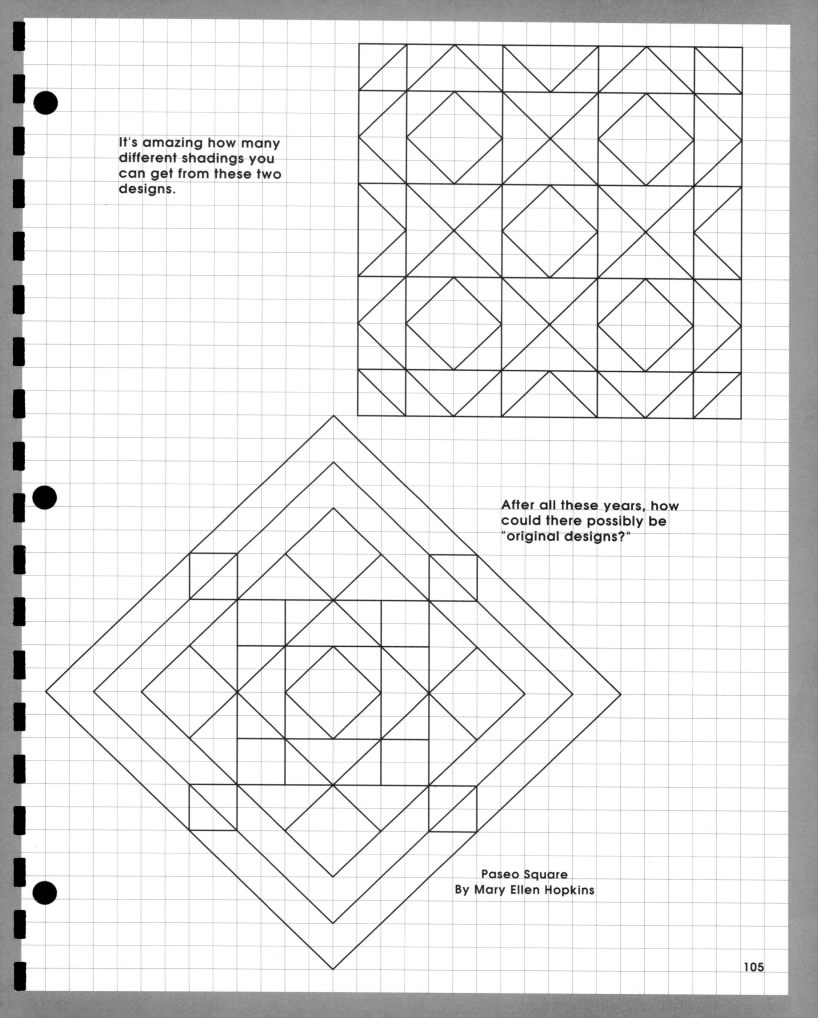

It's amazing how many
different shadings you
can get from these two
designs.

After all these years, how
could there possibly be
"original designs?"

Paseo Square
By Mary Ellen Hopkins

105

Variations, continued

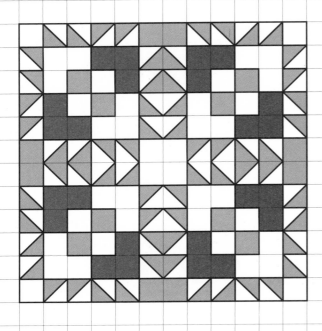

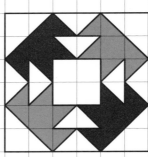

Double-T

This pattern is made up of the repeat of the Double-T block in positive and negative.

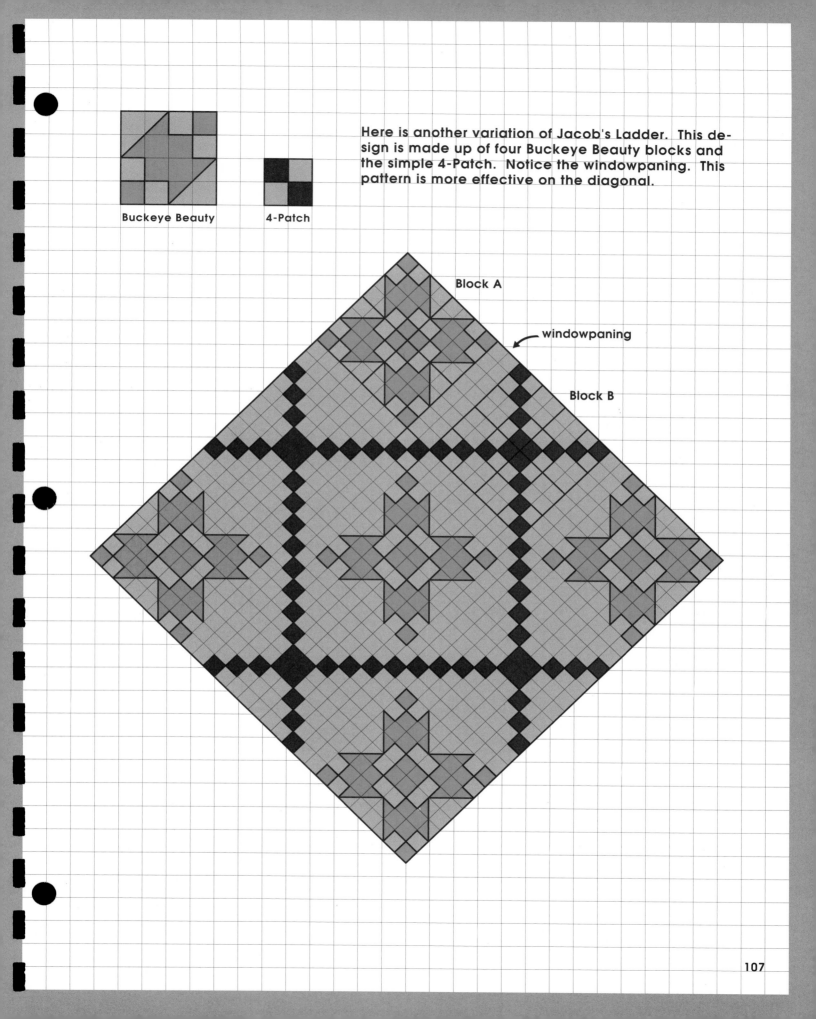

Buckeye Beauty

4-Patch

Here is another variation of Jacob's Ladder. This design is made up of four Buckeye Beauty blocks and the simple 4-Patch. Notice the windowpaning. This pattern is more effective on the diagonal.

Block A

windowpaning

Block B

107

Cleaning Up

Remember that "cleaning up" is achieved by dropping out some design areas. The dotted line in Block A suggests the shapes for the corner fill-ins. Now that I have dropped them out, isn't it a more interesting pattern?

Block A   Block B

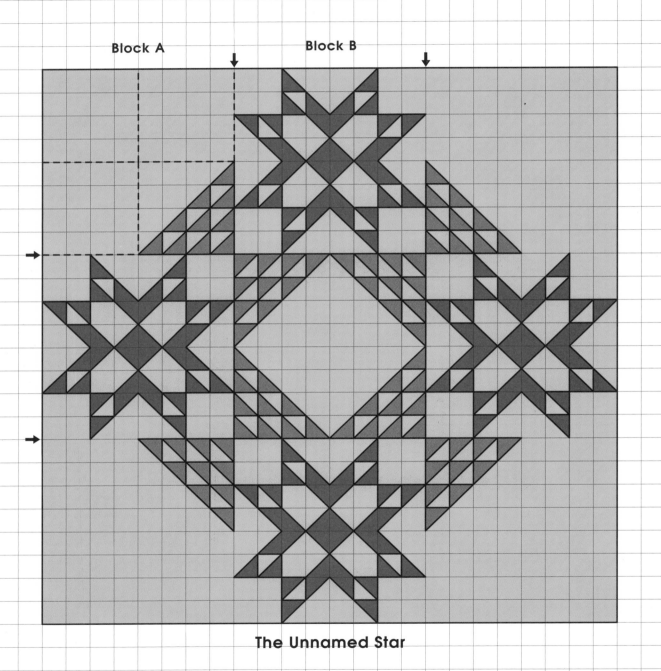

The Unnamed Star

9-Patch Set-Up

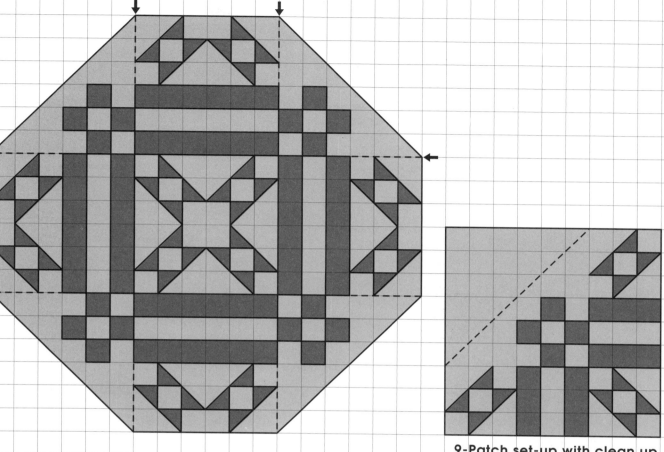

9-Patch set-up with clean up

To get that "art school graduate look," zero in on the Famous Nine-Patch Set-Up.

Nine-Patch is an arrangement of three blocks across and three blocks down, alternating to look like a checkerboard.

In the Famous Nine-Patch Set-Up, the checkerboard may be made from the design in positive/negative color combinations or two different designs.

Draw empty pattern lines; that is, no shading inside your pattern design.

There are three approaches you can take with your empty pattern that will keep people guessing where you studied art.

1. Color it in as if all nine squares are one block (See Joseph's Coat, Page 103).
2. Clean it up. That means, drop out some design areas (see Unnamed Star on the preceding page).
3. Put it on the diagonal. (See Wedding March, pg. 76, also an example of "cleaned up" corners).

You are not, of course, limited to just one choice. Combine any or all of the above for fantastic effects.

This is an ideal graph paper/colored pencil project. Once you get started, you'll probably do a whole series of these designs. Then you will understand why graph paper is a necessity of life.

The Split 9-Patch

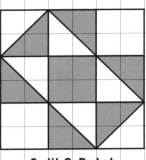

Split 9-Patch
A "2-Bell" block
so let's play with it

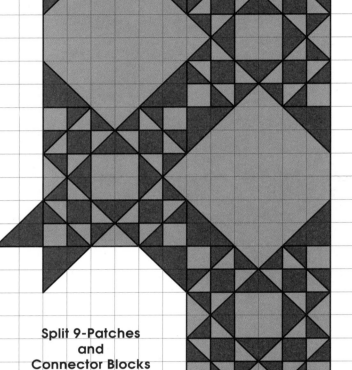

Split 9-Patches
and
Connector Blocks
Make Good Designs

On the Diagonal -
Repeat of 10 Blocks

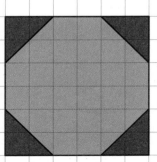

Four Split 9-Patches   Connector Block

And again . . .

The Split
9-Patch

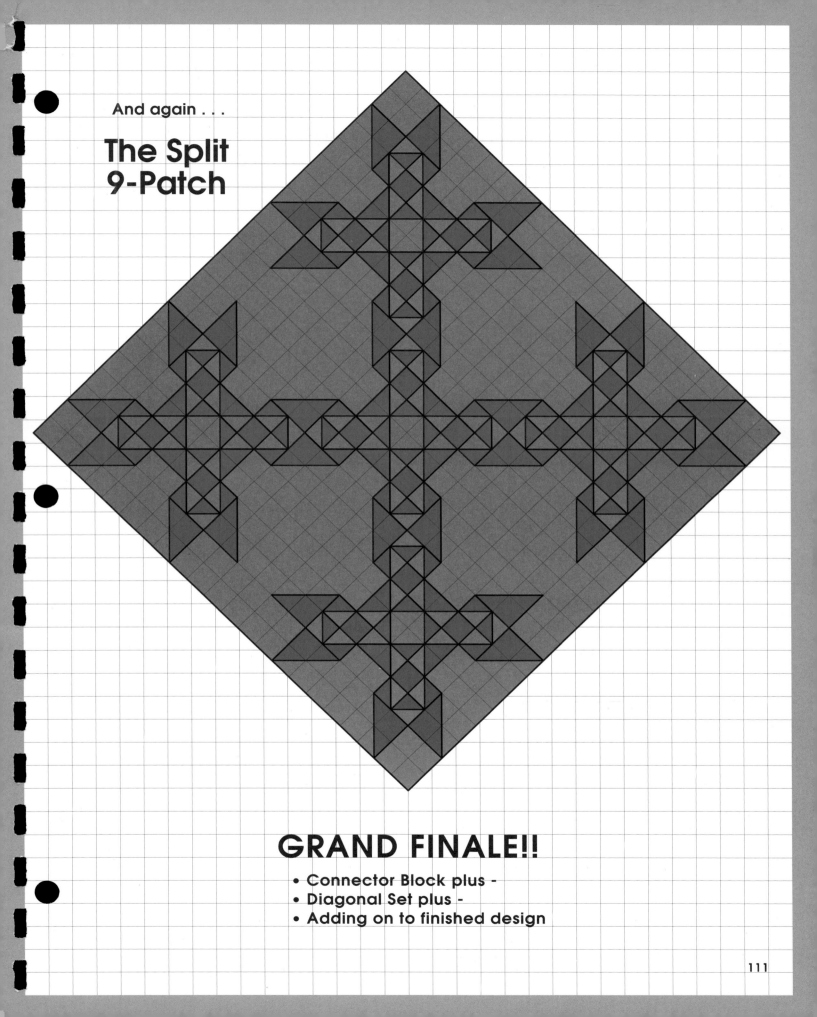

GRAND FINALE!!

- Connector Block plus -
- Diagonal Set plus -
- Adding on to finished design

Block	Number	Page	Block	Number	Page
Air Castle	175	59	(2nd Shading)	349	91
Aircraft	51	43	Double Nine Patch	292	75
Alabama	285	3	Double Pinwheel	179	59
Albany, New York	257	70	Double Sawtooth	110	52
Album	212	62	Double T	162	57
Album	301	78	Dove at my Window	312	82
Alice's Favorite	288	74	Dove-in-the-Window	182	59
Alta Plane	221	64	Dove-in-the-Window	217	64
Amish Pinwhel	42	43	Duck & Ducklings	97	50
Anvil	57	43	Eccentric Star	39	42
Arbor Window	348	91	Eddystone Light	213	62
Arkansas Cross Roads	340	90	Eight Hands Around	255	69
Attic Window	14	39	Enclosed Stars	244	69
Austin, Texas	24	42	English Ivy	148	56
Autumn Leaf	151	56	Eternal Triangle	240	68
Bachelor's Puzzle	69	44	Fair & Square	27	42
Barrister's Block	236	68	Fancy Windmill	241	68
Basket #1	59	43	Fanny's Favorite	266	70
Basket #2	60	43	Fantastic Frame	356	92
Basket	111	52	Feathered Star (simplified)	321	85
Basket	150	56	Five Patch Tree	328	89
Basket of Scraps	116	52	Flower Garden Path	159	57
Basket of Scraps	146	56	Flower Pot	112	52
Baton Rouge, Lousiana	259	70	Flying Bats	282	72
Bear's Paw	214	64	Flying Clouds	269	71
Billie Later's Butterfly	12	39	Flying Dutchman #1	157	57
Birds' Nest	306	79	Flying Dutchman #2	160	57
Birds-in-the-Air #2	164	58	Flying Dutchman	52	43
Birds-in-the-Air	13	39	Flying X	32	42
Birds-in-the-Air	50	43	Fool's Square	103	51
Blackford's Beauty	249	69	Formal Garden	7	39
Blazing Star	316	82	Four Queens	320	85
Boise, Idaho	48	43	Four T's	163	57
Bowtie	56	43	Fox & Geese	72	44
Boxes #1	176	59	Frame	177	59
Brave World	41	42	Framed X	53	43
Broken Path, The	277	71	Georgetown Circle or		
Broken Sugar Bowl	172	58	Crown of Thorns	265	70
Brown Goose	54	43	Georgia	94	50
Buckeye Beauty	81	46	Golden Stairs	11	39
Burnham Squares	319	84	Grandmother's Basket	149	56
Cake Stand	115	52	Grandmother's Choice	106	51
Calico Puzzle	9	39	Grandmother's Dream	315	82
Card Trick	205	62	Grandmother's Favorite	267	70
Carpenter's Wheel Variation	278	71	Grape Basket	114	52
Carson City, Nevada	209	62	Greek Cross	3	39
Casey's Camp	264	70	Greek Cross	218	64
Cat & Mice	184	59	Gretchen	261	70
Cat's Cradle	167	58	H	107	51
Cathedral Window	304	78	Handy Andy	299	78
Children's Delight	109	51	Hartford, Connecticut	303	78
Chinese Puzzle	246	69	Hays Corner	156	57
Christian Cross	351	92	Hens & Chickens	219	64
Christmas Star	314	82	Hill & Valley	180	59
Churn Dash	96	50	Hobby Horse	327	88
Clay's Choice #1	47	43	Hourglass	153	56
Clay's Choice #2	66	44	Hovering Hawks	49	43
Columbus, Ohio	358	38	Homestead	323	88
Contrary Wife	165	58	Indian Hatchet	242	68
County Line Waves	283	72	Indian Puzzle	37	42
Crazy Anne	93	50	Indian Trails & Irish Puzzle	234	68
Cross & Crown	84	50	Interlaced Blocks	311	82
Cross Roads to Texas	342	90	Irene Gutzeit's Iris Rainbow	279	71
Crosses & Losses	77	45	Jack-in-the-Box	82	50
Crow's Foot	243	68	Jack-in-the Pulpit	262	70
Crown of Thorns	107	51	Jackson, Mississippi	289	74
Cube Lattice	82	48	Jefferson City, Missouri	145	56
Cut Glass Dish	204	62	Jewels	18	39
Delectable Mountains	237	68	Jewels in a Frame	232	68
Devil's Claw	238	68	July 4th	30	42
Double Links	189	60	Kansas Troubles	235	68
Diamond Star	254	69	Katie's Favorite	305	79
Domino & Square			Katrina's Flowers		
(1st Shading)	347	91	by Ellen Jensen	324	88